Open Scholarship in the Humanities

Open Scholarship in the Humanities

Paul Longley Arthur and Lydia Hearn

BLOOMSBURY ACADEMIC
LONDON • NEW YORK • OXFORD • NEW DELHI • SYDNEY

BLOOMSBURY ACADEMIC
Bloomsbury Publishing Plc, 50 Bedford Square, London, WC1B 3DP, UK
Bloomsbury Publishing Inc, 1385 Broadway, New York, NY 10018, USA
Bloomsbury Publishing Ireland, 29 Earlsfort Terrace, Dublin 2, D02 AY28, Ireland

BLOOMSBURY, BLOOMSBURY ACADEMIC and the Diana logo are trademarks of
Bloomsbury Publishing Plc

First published in Great Britain 2024
This paperback edition published 2025

Copyright © Paul Longley Arthur and Lydia Hearn, 2024

Paul Longley Arthur and Lydia Hearn have asserted their right under the Copyright, Designs
and Patents Act, 1988, to be identified as the Authors of this work.

For legal purposes the Acknowledgments on p. xi constitute an
extension of this copyright page.

Cover design: Jess Stevens
Cover image: Jess Stevens

This work is published open access subject to a Creative Commons Attribution-
NonCommercial-NoDerivatives 4.0 International licence (CC BY-NC-ND 4.0, https://crea tive
comm ons.org/licen ses/by-nc-nd/4.0/). You may re-use, distribute, and reproduce this work
in any medium for non-commercial purposes, provided you give attribution to the copyright
holder and the publisher and provide a link to the Creative Commons licence.

Open Access was funded by Edith Cowan University, Australia.

All rights reserved. No part of this publication may be: i) reproduced or transmitted in any form, electronic
or mechanical, including photocopying, recording or by means of any information storage or retrieval
system without prior permission in writing from the publishers; or ii) used or reproduced in any way for
the training, development or operation of artificial intelligence (AI) technologies, including generative
AI technologies. The rights holders expressly reserve this publication from the text and data mining
exception as per Article 4(3) of the Digital Single Market Directive (EU) 2019/790.

Bloomsbury Publishing Plc does not have any control over, or responsibility for, any
third-party websites referred to or in this book. All internet addresses given in this
book were correct at the time of going to press. The author and publisher regret any
inconvenience caused if addresses have changed or sites have ceased to exist,
but can accept no responsibility for any such changes.

A catalogue record for this book is available from the British Library.

A catalog record for this book is available from the Library of Congress.

ISBN: HB: 978-1-3502-3227-3
PB: 978-1-3502-3747-6
ePDF: 978-1-3502-3228-0
eBook: 978-1-3502-3229-7

Typeset by Newgen KnowledgeWorks Pvt. Ltd., Chennai, India

For product safety related questions contact productsafety@bloomsbury.com.

To find out more about our authors and books visit www.bloomsbury.com
and sign up for our newsletters.

Contents

List of Tables	vii
List of Abbreviations	viii
Acknowledgments	xi
About the Authors	xii

Introduction: Unlocking Scholarship		1
1	**Scholarly Communication from Past to Present**	7
	Libraries and the Origins of Scholarly Communication	7
	Learned Societies and the First Journals	8
	The Commercialization of Academic Publishing	10
	Computers and the Internet	12
	Publishing in the Digital Age	13
	The Emergence of Open Scholarship	15
2	**Global Policies Promoting Openness**	19
	International Calls for Open Values	19
	Collaboration for Greater Access	22
	Accelerating the Transition to Open Scholarship	23
	National Government and Funding Agency Mandates	34
3	**Barriers in Implementing Open Scholarship**	37
	Socioeconomic, Cultural, and Equity Divides	37
	Institutional and Policy Barriers	38
	Technological and Operational Obstacles	39
	Financial and Legal Factors	40
	Overcoming Barriers	41
4	**Toward the Open Humanities**	45
	Open Science or Open Humanities?	45
	Open Access Publishing in the Humanities	50
	Collecting, Sustaining, and Sharing Humanities Data	54
	Humanities Infrastructure	56
	Community-Based Open Knowledge	58

5	**Reshaping How Universities Assess Research Impact**	63
	Bibliometrics and Impact Factors	63
	Evaluating Scholarly Work	64
	Altmetrics for Assessment	66
	Open Peer Review	68

Conclusion: Pathways to Action — 71

Notes — 75
Bibliography — 111
Index — 133

Tables

1.1	Different Understandings of Openness	16
2.1	The Vienna Principles: A Vision for Scholarly Communication	24
2.2	Key Events Influencing Scholarly Communication	30
3.1	Barriers to Open Scholarship	42
3.2	The Role of Stakeholders in Promoting Open Practices	43

Abbreviations

AI	artificial intelligence
ALLEA	All European Academies
AmeliCA	Open Knowledge Non-profit Academy-Owned Open Access
APC	article processing charge
ARDC	Australian Research Data Commons
ARPANET	Advanced Research Projects Agency Network
BBB	Budapest Open Access Initiative, Bethesda Statement, and Berlin Declaration
BOAI	Budapest Open Access Initiative
BPC	book processing charge
Canadian HSS Commons	Canadian Humanities and Social Sciences Commons
CARE	collective benefit, authority to control, responsibility, ethics (principles for Indigenous data governance)
CC	Creative Commons
CERN	European Organization for Nuclear Research
CLARIN	Common Language Resources and Technology Infrastructure
COAR	Confederation of Open Access Repositories
DARIAH	Digital Research Infrastructure for the Arts and Humanities
DARTS	discoverable, accessible, reusable, transparent, and sustainable
DAS	data availability statements
DOAB	Directory of Open Access Books
DOAJ	Directory of Open Access Journals
DOI	digital object identifier
DORA	Declaration on Research Assessment
EIFL	Electronic Information for Libraries
EOSC	European Open Science Cloud

E-RIHS	European Research Infrastructure for Heritage Science
FAIR	findable, accessible, interoperable, and reusable
GLAM	galleries, libraries, archives, and museums
G20	Group of Twenty (governments)
HASS	humanities, arts, and social sciences
HuNI	Humanities Networked Infrastructure
ICT	information and communications technology
IFLA	International Federation of Library Associations and Institutions
IP	intellectual property
KSHIP	Knowledge Sharing in Publishing
LA Referencia	Federated Network of Institutional Repositories of Scientific Publications
LIBER	Ligue des Bibliothèques Européennes de Recherche—Association of European Research Libraries
OA	open access
OAI	Open Archives Initiative
OAPEN	Open Access Publishing in European Networks
OCR	optical character recognition
OECD	Organisation for Economic Co-operation and Development
OER	open educational resource
OJS	Open Journal Systems
OKF	Open Knowledge Foundation
OLH	Open Library of Humanities
OpenAIRE	Open Access Infrastructure for Research in Europe
OPERAS	Open Scholarly Communication in the European Research Area for Social Sciences and Humanities
ORCID	Open Researcher and Contributor ID
ORFG	Open Research Funders Group
OS	open science
OSS	open source software
PARADISEC	Pacific and Regional Archive for Digital Sources in Endangered Cultures
PI or PID	persistent identifier
PLOS	Public Library of Science
POSI	Principles of Open Scholarly Infrastructure
Redalyc	Red de Revistas Científicas de América Latina, y El Caribe, España y Portugal

REF	Research Excellence Framework
SADiLaR	South African Centre for Digital Language Resources
SciELO	Scientific Electronic Library Online
SPARC	Scholarly Publishing and Academic Resources Coalition
STEM	science, technology, engineering, and mathematics
TLCMap	Time-Layered Cultural Map
UNESCO	United Nations Educational, Scientific and Cultural Organization

Acknowledgments

We would like to thank all those who generously shared their knowledge of open scholarship during the writing of this book. We have benefited from the insights of colleagues working in many different contexts nationally and internationally in open research, digital humanities, and related fields. Numerous collaborators and mentors have in various ways and at different times informed our thinking on opportunities for openness in the digital era. At Bloomsbury, we especially thank Ben Doyle for his encouragement and support. Philippa Tucker contributed invaluable research and editorial assistance. We are also grateful to Bob Land, who copyedited, proofread, and indexed the text. We particularly acknowledge Edith Cowan University, Western Australia, for providing a strong institutional environment for this study.

About the Authors

Paul Longley Arthur is Vice-Chancellor's Professorial Research Fellow and Chair in Digital Humanities and Social Sciences at Edith Cowan University, Western Australia. He speaks and publishes widely on major challenges and changes facing twenty-first-century society, from the global impacts of technology on communication, culture, and identity to migration and human rights.
https://orcid.org/0000-0002-1494-0533

Lydia Hearn has over forty years of research experience in Australia, Colombia, Egypt, the Netherlands, the UK, and the United States. Much of her focus has been on open collaborative development aimed at translating policy into practice through equity and inclusion.
https://orcid.org/0000-0003-2554-156X

Introduction: Unlocking Scholarship

In today's rapidly changing world of information and communications technology (ICT), openness is transforming how knowledge is created and shared. The potential for unrestricted global circulation of groundbreaking new ideas and discoveries represents one of the most valuable opportunities for our digital future. Billions of people have internet-connected devices with the capacity to instantly retrieve a vast wealth of material online, offering practically limitless possibilities for access to information and data—provided it is readily findable and freely available.

This book provides an overview of key issues, directions, and priorities for open scholarship at a time when its principles are being almost universally accepted as a paradigm-shifting advance in the production and dissemination of knowledge, but when in practice it is facing multiple impediments to successful adoption. Open scholarship in the humanities and sciences is driven by the same fundamental principles, so any discussion of humanities needs to be set within the overall open scholarship movement. However, there are significant differences in approach, implementation, and potential benefits in the two arenas.

Open scholarship, from its historical origins to the present, is examined here with a particular emphasis on the humanities. Also referred to as *open knowledge* or *open research*, *open scholarship* "encompasses open access, open data, open science, open educational resources, and all other forms of openness in the scholarly and research environment," using digital formats, tools, standards, and infrastructures.[1] The open scholarship movement seeks to reshape long-standing traditions of scholarly communication by encouraging more accessible, participatory, interactive, ethical, and transparent approaches, and to involve far wider and more diverse publics.[2] Aligned with broader open society initiatives in government, education, health, justice, and many other fields, a central tenet of open scholarship is its call for more equitable and inclusive societies.

By enhancing public engagement with academic research through knowledge translation, it aims to "foster a culture of greater scientific education and literacy,"[3] strengthen national and international collaboration, and enrich the lives and livelihoods of people everywhere.[4]

The conventional model of scholarly communication reinforced the authority of printed documents, with a well-established publishing paradigm that validated new knowledge—not only controlling and managing its flow but also limiting its readership. Open scholarship challenged this model, transforming it from being closed and print-centric to open and network driven.[5] It embraced the sharing of outputs and data. The aim was to unlock the doors that traditionally kept knowledge hidden from public view and to make findings more discoverable and usable among researchers, organizations, and the community for maximum value and impact.[6] Over the past two decades of continuous digital innovation, open scholarship has changed how research is conducted and communicated. The movement has gained significant momentum, accelerating dramatically in recent years with the support of universities, governments, funders, publishers, libraries, the ICT sector, and the public.

There are many motives for openness, such as improving academic publishing arrangements for more responsive and cost-effective dissemination of research, pooling expertise to find solutions to global problems and for sustainable development, ensuring better accountability and equity in research, and transitioning to fully digital publication and data-sharing platforms.[7] Crucially, in an era of ever-growing reliance on online information in daily life, extending the audience for scholarly communication into the public domain and offering trusted perspectives and proven evidence are essential for countering fake news and other contemporary "crises of misinformation."[8]

The initial focus of the open scholarship movement in the early years of the twenty-first century was on unrestricted open access (OA) to published resources—not requiring user payment, uninhibited by copyright constraints, and with few licensing limitations for reuse, but, importantly, continuing to provide clear authorship attribution. In what was a radical departure, its proponents championed principles of free and unimpeded public utilization of the results of academic inquiry "to remove barriers to all legitimate scholarly uses for scholarly literature."[9] Research findings and data can now be published or made available online through a wide array of OA journals and institutional repositories rather than being hidden behind restrictive publication paywalls, increasing their reach and relevance. Yet the focus of open scholarship has expanded over time and today covers much more than just OA to publications or final outputs. The concept of open scholarship includes making research data and metadata more visible and openly obtainable for use and reuse. In addition to storing or archiving of data by a researcher for their own or an organization's primary use, open data allows free access for secondary analysis, verification, and authentication, and serves as a basis for further research and development.[10] The emerging vision for open scholarship is even broader, foreseeing "a fully interconnected global scholarly ecosystem" with a "wide variety of open publishing models, underpinned by linked, well curated, interoperable software, data and research articles,"[11] comprising "the entire process of scholarship," including "grant proposals, data, software, educational materials and methods, and research evaluation."[12] Achieving these goals will require infrastructure to link open collections and archives, digital libraries, data repositories, and educational resources, and implementing open licenses, access policies, and open peer review, among other approaches[13]—so that research is as discoverable, accessible, reusable, transparent, and sustainable (DARTS) as possible.[14]

Numerous government and nongovernmental organizations are expediting the worldwide transition to open scholarship. National and international policy directives have affirmed the importance of presenting research outputs in findable, accessible, interoperable, and reusable (FAIR) ways, and with data made more easily available to "connect academics with one another and the communities they serve."[15] The higher education and research sector is under pressure to take responsibility for enabling openness in knowledge production and distribution at all stakeholder levels. Universities are slowly moving toward a future where universal access to research is a core principle. Countless other participants—particularly funding agencies—have now also introduced open policies, with these forming part of their grant conditions. Fundamentally, open scholarship supports the democratization of the digital environment by inviting greater engagement between the producers and users of research.[16] It emphasizes civic participation and co-construction of knowledge to foster collective intelligence, including through citizen science and citizen humanities.[17] Social scholarship, facilitated by the social web—social networking services and social media—can elicit such involvement and user contributions, generating new dialogue and critique.[18]

Making research as open and available as feasible, however, demands further major-scale, coordinated change across every part of the system, and many barriers currently exist. Globally, the persistent lack of equitable access to academic research is a widening socioeconomic divide.[19] Open practices are being adopted unevenly among countries and regions, within and between institutions, as well as at the individual and discipline levels.[20] Researchers, administrators, librarians, and ICT specialists are voicing concerns about the scarcity of appropriate infrastructure, investment, and training, and the limited incentives and recognition for those who do advocate openness.[21] University evaluation and ranking continue to be determined largely according to traditional bibliometrics, that is, through publication and citation analysis rather than in terms of public engagement and benefit. Current reward structures do not encourage open practices and often actively disincentivize them.[22] Internationally, universities and research institutions are hard-pressed to afford or retain OA to publicly funded research due to the increasing costs of digital scholarship.[23] A clear gap is present between policy commitment to open scholarship and its successful implementation, as evidenced by a range of measures, including irregular uptake of open publishing models.[24]

The success of open scholarship initiatives will depend on building further international commitment and advocating common values and practical actions to overcome these and other obstacles. There is an urgent need for partnership and cooperation between all stakeholders to address multilevel barriers to policy alignment and application of open scholarship—across university faculties and with funders, government agencies, peak bodies, civic groups, and industry to attend to institutional, technical, financial, and legal problems in the implementation, sustainability, and effectiveness of open practices.

In view of the notable emphasis on open scholarship in the sciences to date, moves have been underway to specifically promote openness in the humanities—increasingly referred to as the *open humanities*.[25] This book identifies key opportunities and challenges for open scholarship with a focus on the humanities, showing why and how the global research community must work together more effectively for meaningful change. When considered from the perspective of the humanities, social and equity issues come to the fore. Many aspects of open scholarship described in this book apply across disciplines, but the humanities are particularly well positioned to address issues of diversity and inclusion, which is a framing theme throughout. Because of the slower uptake of open practices, there are also real opportunities for humanities research to reach wider audiences for greater influence and impact.[26]

Chapter 1 gives a wide-ranging overview of the broader historical context in which open scholarship has emerged, reflecting on the history of scholarly communication, beginning with the first libraries of the ancient world. Topics covered include the role of new technology in the dissemination of knowledge, the establishment of learned societies and academic journals, the introduction of commercial academic publishing models, and changing copyright regulation, leading to the emergence of the open scholarship movement and OA publishing.

Chapter 2 begins by reviewing the foundational policy statements and declarations calling for OA to research publications and data—global calls that challenged a model of scholarly communication dominated by the commercial publishing sector. The text then traces the changes that have occurred over the past two decades, showing the shifting focus from providing access to research literature toward more progressive calls for the implementation of FAIR principles for the open dissemination of all types of research and data.

Chapter 3 explores barriers to implementing open scholarship. The discussion opens with overarching sociocultural and equity concerns that existing digital divides are being reinforced or widened. It then turns to current issues in the university context, focusing on institutional and systemic obstacles, which include the complexity of the academic system, shortage of incentives, insufficient training, the fragmented and siloed nature of some open initiatives, limited advocacy for change, and lack of dialogue and collaboration, together with ongoing issues around intellectual property and copyright that have slowed the uptake of open solutions. The chapter illustrates the roles that stakeholders, from individuals to institutions, can play in overcoming these barriers.

Chapter 4 focuses on key issues for humanities open scholarship. It describes how humanities disciplines broadly differ from those of the sciences in terms of the way scholarship is conducted, how outputs are rated and valued, and in their philosophies and approaches to knowledge. Recognizing that open humanities is frequently subsumed under open science, the discussion investigates multiple factors that have contributed to the slower development and uptake of openness in the humanities, many of them stemming from the transposition of science-based conventions and measures directly to the humanities where they may be less appropriate. The chapter explores the different traditions of collaboration and publication in the "two cultures" and how these also influence levels of motivation and investment in open resources and practices. Another point of difference is in the nature of data and their management. The final sections focus on the development of humanities research infrastructure and on social and community-based forms of knowledge creation.

Chapter 5 investigates ways to give greater recognition to the societal impact and benefit of research in addition to conventional performance and ranking metrics that have limited the uptake of open scholarship. Universities continue to place a high value on encouraging publications in prestigious journals and books that are assessed and judged using traditional bibliometric indicators. The discussion critiques universities' established approaches to measuring academic performance and considers drivers for change. Topics covered include the use of altmetrics and open peer review. Diversification of modes of research assessment, including involving community stakeholders and end users, may offer new means for universities to evaluate the effectiveness of research and scholarly communication, while encouraging them to become more open.

1

Scholarly Communication from Past to Present

This chapter discusses key stages in the evolution of scholarly communication. From the first libraries to the establishment of learned societies and their journals, advances in printing technologies and papermaking machines, through to the beginnings of copyright law and later the commercialization of academic publishing, this background sets the scene for the lead-up to the internet age and the start of the open access movement. It shows how international calls for open scholarship were supported through legal changes brought about by Creative Commons and the establishment of institutional repositories, explains their influence on publishers in developing open access publication models, and reviews understandings of the concept of openness, outlining motivations for open practices.

Libraries and the Origins of Scholarly Communication

The history of scholarly communication can be traced back thousands of years to the first libraries of the ancient world, including in Persian, Chinese, Egyptian, Greek, and Roman civilizations. They gathered, compiled, and organized information about society, documenting and sustaining human knowledge and heritage, and fostering learning. Responsible for preservation and access to their vast wealth of resources, libraries have played a vital role in enabling scholarship and education.[1] Their collections are historical records of human inquiry and creativity across cultures and time, and a foundation for research in all disciplines, but especially for the humanities, with its focus on writing, languages, and history. Where they still exist, the earliest rare and fragile texts are invaluable protectors of the legacy of past societies.[2]

Over time, information has been preserved and passed on using different media and systems for collection, storage, and distribution, with new technologies playing a role at each stage in democratizing knowledge through widening access.[3] A notable early collection dates from the seventh century BCE in Nineveh, present-day northern Iraq, when the Assyrian king Ashurbanipal ordered the systematic acquisition and production of thousands of cuneiform texts on clay and wooden tablets for his personal use and imperial purposes.[4] The Great Library of Alexandria, Egypt, one of the largest and a center of learning, established around 300 BCE, is known to have contained huge numbers of papyrus rolls and pioneered alphabetical ordering of its holdings. A century later, in the Library of Pergamum in present-day Turkey, founded around 197–159 BCE, manuscripts were written on parchment, which was established as a thriving local industry. The imperial collection of the Former Han dynasty of 206 BCE–9 CE, often described as the first Chinese library, is the earliest known to have a catalog, ordered chronologically and by category for reference.[5] Textual criticism and editing initially developed as a way to systematically describe and order very large quantities of manuscripts and books.[6]

Through much of their history, libraries housed a scarce, safeguarded resource,[7] only available to the wealthy and the privileged, literate elite. Most collections were held privately, limiting public access, and as such represented power and influence. The history of public libraries dates to Roman times, but the Malatestiana Library in Cesena, Italy, opened in 1454, is known to have been the first civic library in Europe to make both secular and religious texts fully open to the public, and it is now the world's oldest extant public library.[8] This was also a time of major advances in printing technology. Movable type, which had originated in China, was introduced to Europe with Gutenberg's printing press around the mid-fifteenth century. The production of handwritten books by scribes in monasteries in the Middle Ages had been slow and the results not widely accessible, due in part to the laborious process and also low literacy rates. The advent of printing allowed multiple copies of scholarly works to be made and shared, leading to increasing circulation of knowledge, growing literacy, and an expanding role for libraries.

Learned Societies and the First Journals

Learned societies were founded in Europe in the 1300s–1600s to bring together scholarly communities and develop disciplines. Such societies fostered extensive networks of disciplinary or professional expertise to encourage interaction and overcome secrecy so that their fellows could learn from and expand on each other's work.[9] Yet until at least the fifteenth century, academia mostly constituted a closed community, with little emphasis on reaching wider publics and, in the absence of copyright laws, a reluctance to share knowledge for fear of ideas being usurped.[10] It was not until the 1660s that the notion of a published journal to inform and update members of learned societies of new discoveries and ideas gained support. The *Journal des Sçavans* and *Philosophical Transactions* (the latter the world's longest continuously published academic journal) were both established in 1665.[11] These journals of the Académie des Science in Paris and the Royal Society of London for Improving Natural Knowledge (now the Royal Society) were a means for the serial publication of letter excerpts; detailed accounts of original observations, experiments, and inventions; and reviews and summaries of recently published scholarly books.

The Royal Society fervently argued that knowledge could only be advanced by the transparent and evidence-based exchange of ideas and debate for improved validation and understanding.[12] To this end, the society's secretary Henry Oldenburg introduced the practice of sending submitted manuscripts to other scholars who could judge their quality and suitability before publication—later formalized as "peer review," which has remained the norm for evaluation of academic articles to this day.[13] Oldenburg described the journal as an avenue for learned thinkers to "be invited and encouraged to search, try, and find out new things, impart their knowledge to one another, and contribute what they can to the Grand design of improving natural knowledge, and perfecting all Philosophical Arts, and Sciences."[14] During the Enlightenment period, more learned societies and numerous universities were founded throughout Europe and in the Americas, with many dedicated to particular disciplines or branches of learning, and each producing their own journals. By the end of the eighteenth century, hundreds of such periodicals existed,[15] and they soon came to be central to the "social contract of science" to share discoveries more widely.[16] With only minor changes since their introduction, academic journals remain the primary vehicle for scholarly communication.

The first modern copyright laws for printers and publishers were those introduced in England in 1710, under the Statute of Anne, named for Queen Anne.[17] These laws were aimed at promoting learning and curtailing copying and claiming credit for the original expression of ideas by granting individuals the sole right to decide and consent to whether and by whom their work could be printed, published, or otherwise reproduced. Also known as "An Act for the

Encouragement of Learning," this statute gave authors the right for fourteen years (twenty-one years for the protection of those books already in print), with an automatic right to a further fourteen years if still living, after which the work would enter the public domain.[18] This had the effect of reinforcing author entitlements and reducing publishers' control through a legally binding agreement while also assisting and regulating the spread of knowledge and new ideas.[19] Ongoing development of printing techniques led to much quicker dissemination of information to a growing academic community. Yet even with advances in print technology, the high cost of paper limited the spread of printed works until the nineteenth century with the invention of the Fourdrinier machine in 1806.[20] By the mid-nineteenth century, the widespread use of pulp and papermaking machines made it relatively inexpensive to quickly produce large quantities of books, articles, and other publications, and paper arguably became "the chief industrial product of the nineteenth century."[21] In the process, highly competitive modern printing monopolies emerged.

The Commercialization of Academic Publishing

Increasing investment in and expansion of research capacity worldwide in the twentieth century following waves of industrial and technological revolution led ultimately to the development of modern computing and telecommunications. Pivotal shifts in scholarly communication occurred following the Second World War with the expansion of higher education,[22] extensive professionalization of research, and growth of government funding in North America and Western Europe in particular.[23] Support provided to US universities at the time was part of the nation's continuing drive to be a leading world power, strengthened by scientific research.[24] In his well-known report *Science: The Endless Frontier*, Vannevar Bush, president of the Carnegie Institute, called for a substantial expansion of government financing.[25] This led to the creation of the National Science Foundation, which remains an independent agency for federal research funding and has served as a model for numerous international governments to build scientific capacity. Bush is also known for his speculative essay on the potential for an electro-optical "Memex" device and information system that would extend human memory, a vision that was a precursor to the development of hypertext.[26]

With the proliferation of academic publications following the Second World War, learned societies and university presses were pressured to maintain a balance between journal prestige and making articles widely available and released on time. Few such presses had been financially profitable; the majority were sustained by university libraries and sponsors of learned societies.[27] Bush insisted that academics be left to freely direct their own research agendas, arguing that curiosity-driven inquiry would give rise to unanticipated solutions and benefits over time.[28] This model, encouraging autonomy and self-governance, meant that university researchers were not required to have their work judged by policymakers or the general public.[29] Academic boards dominated by elite scholars would increasingly consider research excellence in terms of publications in top-tiered journals and books.

It was in this environment that Robert Maxwell, director of the Butterworth-Springer company in London, saw the opportunity to change academic publishing into a commercial venture. He bought the company he renamed Pergamon Press in 1951.[30] Maxwell observed that universities employed academics who wrote articles and books, vetted and peer-reviewed colleagues' research, and served on editorial boards that oversaw the publishing process—in other words, much of the work in this industry was being done for free.[31] University libraries then paid to purchase the published works. While economists would consider this a dysfunctional market for academia, commercial publishers saw many opportunities. Maxwell identified the potential to take control of this market, opening numerous journals focused on topics of growing interest and new subdisciplines, and offering these through subscription to university libraries rather than to individuals and learned societies.[32] He entertained leading foreign academics to secure international markets, with exclusive contracts for scholars to publish their work in English, thus serving a vastly larger group of consumers. Pergamon's publishing became highly profitable, and its approach was soon copied and diversified by long-standing firms such as Elsevier, Macmillan, and Taylor and Francis, which either launched new journals or acquired existing ones from smaller publishers.[33]

Copyright laws were central to the success of this commercial academic publishing model, giving exclusive rights to the authors of the original work for a limited time, or until they elected to grant their rights to another entity. This latter component enabled publishing companies to establish a contractual system whereby authors assigned exclusive rights to their work and its distribution, while also allowing publishers to maximize profits.[34] Academics today continue to give away their copyrights as a condition of publishing in prestigious scholarly outlets that certify the quality of their work, with the expectation that it will be disseminated to a desired audience.[35]

Computers and the Internet

The digital revolution of the second half of the twentieth century pointed to the remarkable prospect of future online global connectivity and information access. Universities were early adopters of computing technology, from the time of the first large-scale production of computers starting in the 1950s. Development of common programming languages and operating systems led to source code being readily shared.[36] In the late 1960s, the Advanced Research Projects Agency Network (ARPANET) pioneered node-to-node connectivity from one computer to another via a single network. With the mass production of personal computers from the 1970s and the development of worldwide telecommunications systems linked through networked infrastructure, it became possible to transmit more effectively over greater distances. As technology development continued, multiple networks were formed, supported through open protocols and standards for how data could be sent and received. This system of internetworking came to be referred to as the "internet." Having initially been used for communication across a limited number of research and defense institutions in the United States, the development by Tim Berners-Lee in the late 1980s of the Hypertext Transfer Protocol and World Wide Web opened up the internet. When the Web was put into the public domain as an open standard by the European Organization for Nuclear Research (CERN) in 1993, it quickly evolved and expanded.[37] The prospect of ideas being exchanged in real time showed the potential for online information to reach very wide specialist and nonspecialist audiences, and so "allow the full technical power of the Internet to be brought to bear on education."[38] The early Web endorsed openness of expression, free speech, and self-publishing.[39] This was particularly liberating for the humanities, where the barriers to publishing research findings, narratives, ideas, memoirs, and historical records had been all but insurmountable for individuals who did not have an established reputation in their field.[40]

The free software movement was an important precursor to and model for open access (OA) publishing and open scholarship.[41] During the 1960s and 1970s, almost all software was produced following principles of openness and collaboration, rather than commodification. But as operating systems and programming languages advanced, Unix and various commercial groups started to incorporate software into the costs of hardware products. Many of the then so-called hobbyists or hackers were not happy with this commercial push, and in 1983 computer programmer Richard Stallman launched the free software movement for the sharing of source code between programmers and users. This included Stallman's GNU project to produce a complete Unix-compatible operating system and distribute it free of charge.[42] The GNU manifesto outlined the importance and purpose of free software.[43] To support the movement, Stallman pioneered the concept of "copyleft" (from the term *copyright*) and championed the first general public licenses to preserve the legal right to use, study, modify, and redistribute software free of charge and without restriction.[44] He saw this as an important social stance for freedom of information and emphasized the term *free* as in "libre" rather than "gratis"—in other words, "to be free" rather than "for free."[45] The principles and values of free and open source software (OSS) have become closely linked with those of open scholarship and are put in practice by software communities that develop many of the advanced systems and tools for academics to make their work openly available.[46]

Yet, just as the digital environment was potentially offering vastly improved access to and sharing of academic research, lucrative publishers were gaining increasing power and control over the purchase costs and dissemination of these outputs.[47] From the 1970s, the price of library subscriptions to publications and the purchase price of books began rising above the rate of inflation. This continued for over thirty years, while library budgets remained relatively static.[48] Project Gutenberg, the first digital library, had been founded in 1971 to make e-books available to the public at little or no cost, and while it was innovative, very few people then had access to computers.[49] Most learned societies and university presses were unable to compete with the major international printing conglomerates. While some prominent institutions adopted fundraising strategies, smaller learned societies eventually entered into copublishing arrangements with the major commercial companies that provided them with sales, editing, and new technology services.[50]

Publishing in the Digital Age

During this crisis the OA movement started, driven by librarians' concerns that commercial publishers were restricting access to scholarly publications and driving up costs just when digital technology was transforming possibilities for more affordable sharing of research outputs. The digital packages that publishers were introducing offered researchers instant virtual access to a much greater variety of literature, while also making this information more discoverable. But this came at a high cost for institutions. The situation was exacerbated in the late

1990s and early 2000s as publishers started to introduce "big deal" multiyear packages offering library subscriptions to a large market share of their serial journals, including online content, with set annual price increases.[51] In 1998, the Scholarly Publishing and Academic Resources Coalition (SPARC), an alliance of academic libraries and other organizations, was established to seek alternatives. Many were arguing that research findings should not be treated as a commodity to be sold but be the public property of those who pay taxes that support academic salaries and expenses. A range of key initiatives at this time—including the launch of the open source Open Journal Systems (OJS) platform (developed by a group of universities that founded the Public Knowledge Project in 1998)[52] and the establishment of the Open Archives Initiative (OAI) in 1999[53]—were followed by a series of major international statements from 2002 calling for unrestricted online access to research outputs (see Chapter 2).

Creative Commons (CC) was established in 2001 as a nonprofit organization providing licenses and tools to grant copyright permissions for academic and creative works.[54] Since then, a choice of CC licenses has been developed for authors to specify how works can be used or shared, with the six most regularly used allowing different degrees of freedom.[55] The most permissive is the CC BY license, which gives end users all the legal prerogatives that copyright holders have, provided they acknowledge the creator. At the other end of the scale, the CC BY-NC-ND license requires that in addition to recognizing the creator, any free use and distribution must be for noncommercial purposes and in unadapted form. Creative Commons is recognized for breaking new ground by rethinking the institutional, practical, and legal frameworks required for works to be circulated more freely, countering what was perceived as an increasingly powerful and constraining "permission culture."[56]

Around the same time, a range of OA publication models were being pioneered. What are known as the "green" and "gold" options have become the most commonly used. Green—the original vision for OA—calls on authors to self-archive a version of their work in either a discipline-based or university institutional repository.[57] Preprints can generally be made openly available immediately, but postprints or author-accepted manuscripts usually have a specified embargo period.[58] The first green model platform was arXiv, which began in the early 1990s as an archive for physics preprints.[59] Since then, institutional repositories have evolved to enable universities to offer free access to research outputs and data. They can host a wide variety of materials, including preprint and postprint articles, conference papers, theses, manuscripts, reports, course notes, and digital assets such as images and multimedia, as well as research data.[60]

The gold OA option allows publications to be made openly available immediately in their final published form. However, this typically requires authors or their institutions to pay the publisher article processing charges (APCs) or book processing charges (BPCs). While this approach can be costly, the benefit of this OA model is that academics can choose preferred publishers to make their research openly accessible. However, as publishers in turn impose subscription fees on universities for journal packages, this arrangement essentially results in publishers being paid twice.[61] While initially many of the traditional publishing companies were wary of OA, after testing the gold model, international conglomerates saw the potential for this approach and are now offering OA journals alongside their traditional journals, thus maintaining control of the industry.[62]

A further OA option, the "diamond model," first named in 2012, requires no fees from the author or reader.[63] Sometimes called "platinum," "cooperative," "noncommercial," or referred to as the "open access commons model,"[64] publications in this category are not supported by commercial publishers. They tend to be more prevalent in the humanities and social sciences; as they serve "a fine-grained variety of generally small-scale, multilingual, and multicultural scholarly communities, these journals and platforms embody the concept of bibliodiversity."[65] Yet they may also generally lack the recognition and visibility that international publishers provide.[66]

The Emergence of Open Scholarship

Beyond the call for open and unrestricted access to scholarly outputs, the open scholarship movement from the start of the twenty-first century has sought to uphold fundamental human rights of equity and justice, contributing to "building a future in which research and education in every part of the world are that much more free to flourish."[67] Extending on Ernest Boyer's foundational discourse around universities' need to focus on solutions to the most pressing civic, social, economic, and moral problems,[68] openness offers a purposeful way for universities to bridge the gap between makers and users of research—that is, the "elite" academic world and civil society—through increased public exchange and accountability.[69] Key elements of open scholarship explored in various ways throughout this book include democratization, pragmatism and transparency, infrastructure, measurement, and public good.[70]

Open scholarship has developed in various ways and has multiple meanings (see Table 1.1).[71] The field and its practices are multifaceted and dynamic. At

Table 1.1 Different Understandings of Openness

Openness as free, unrestricted access to information and research	Openness can be understood as providing free, immediate online access to, and largely unrestricted use of, information by anyone with an internet connection, regardless of location. This can include sharing research outputs and data, methods, and tools. Using findable, accessible, interoperative, and reusable (FAIR) principles, free, unhindered access can ensure that scholarly works reach wider audiences.
Openness of preprints and gray literature	Openness can involve OA to electronic preprint and postprint versions of publications, and to gray literature, such as government reports and reviews, that fall outside traditional publishing channels.
Openness as freedom of inquiry	Openness relates to rights of access to information held by government and publicly funded research organizations, allowing for public scrutiny. This entails the legal right of citizens to freely access any such materials unless there are reasonable grounds for safeguarding privacy.
Openness of educational resources	Openness encompasses the sharing of educational and outreach materials, making universities more engaged with wider society. Resources such as lecture notes, courses, and even textbooks can be made openly available online and shared with self-learners and community members.
Openness for preservation and sustainability	Openness is regarded as essential for the preservation and sustainability of all forms of knowledge for the global community. Digitization and digital collections can provide an enduring presence of world information and a foundation for further research.
Openness through a digital, networked environment	Openness is progressively viewed as a way of leveraging the power of networked online communities through engagement and knowledge sharing. By enabling more interactive, open communication, the digital environment can facilitate and incentivize new forms of participation and co-creation to reach far broader publics.
Openness as authorship rights	Openness can be understood in terms of authorship rights to academic and creative works, acknowledging ownership and giving control for a set period of time or until authors elect to make works freely accessible to others. Authors can also self-archive and share their work through open disciplinary and institutional repositories.
Openness for governance and transparency	Openness is aligned with ethical and inclusive governance, transparency, and public engagement, and is regarded as a way of ensuring accountability and responsibility.
Openness as user rights	Openness increasingly indicates not just free access but also the right to reuse, study, modify, and redistribute copies of works in the public domain. By using CC licenses, research outputs can be more easily found, cited, and utilized for societal benefit rather than being kept locked behind paywalls.

Openness for the democratization of knowledge	Openness is seen as central to the creation of an open society that offers opportunities for a more productive, universal design and use of knowledge. This can provide pathways for more just, equitable, and inclusive access to new ideas and information, for finding solutions to global problems, and for sustainable development.

the policy level, this translates into different emphases in openness.[72] Open access, open research, open knowledge, open science, open humanities, open society, and other related terms all imply differences in the focus and purpose of being open. For many, openness in scholarship refers to the use of digital platforms to make research fully and immediately available to the academic community and the general public. For others, openness is considered as a form of freedom of inquiry.[73] In this context, openness relates to rights of access to information held by government and publicly funded research organizations, allowing for public scrutiny. Openness can also refer to open educational resources (OERs) such as syllabi and lesson plans, presentation slides, lecture videos and podcasts, worksheets, and even textbooks, which can be freely accessed, revised, reused, translated, and otherwise adapted. Openness has a role to play in preserving knowledge in sustainable ways in the networked environment. It can relate to authorship rights to academic and creative works, and is also aligned with ethical governance, transparency, and public engagement, including user rights.[74] Yet for others, openness is about democratizing knowledge through enhancing cooperation to make society more just and equitable, through increased participation, inclusivity, and recognition of diversity.[75]

The history of scholarly communication that has been discussed in this chapter provides a foundation for understanding current values associated with openness in research. It illustrates a complex interplay of factors, including changing academic practices, the move from private to public knowledge, increased literacy and circulation of information, development of new technologies, and the pressures of commercial interests. The next chapter traces how the early open scholarship movement was formalized and gained momentum through a series of landmark statements and policies that led to shared international principles to prompt decisive change in scholarly communication practices.

2

Global Policies Promoting Openness

This chapter reviews international policy development advocating open scholarship. The momentum toward openness started in the 1990s, but not until the early twenty-first century did pragmatic and progressive global policies for open access and scholarship begin to gain extensive support. Since then, there have been numerous global calls to action and policy statements formulated to champion open practices. The discussion progresses through a series of key declarations and charters pointing to changing and expanding notions of openness in wide-ranging contexts, from the influential initiatives of the early 2000s through to the United Nations Educational, Scientific and Cultural Organization (UNESCO) Recommendation on Open Science in 2021.

International Calls for Open Values

The Budapest Open Access Initiative, the Bethesda Statement on Open Access Publishing, and the Berlin Declaration on Access to Knowledge in the Sciences and Humanities—often referred to together as the "BBB declarations"—are recognized as the foundational international statements promoting openness in scholarly communication.[1] The Budapest Open Access Initiative (BOAI) in 2002 was the first of these, and it continues to influence open scholarship policy today. With a focus on making research literature freely accessible online, the BOAI defined "open access" as

> free availability on the public internet, permitting any users to read, download, copy, distribute, print, search, or link to the full texts of these articles, crawl them for indexing, pass them as data to software, or use them for any other lawful purpose, without financial, legal, or technical barriers other than those inseparable from gaining access to the internet itself.[2]

The BOAI indicated the important role open access (OA) could play in breaking down social and economic divides:

> Removing access barriers to this literature will accelerate research, enrich education, share the learning of the rich with the poor and the poor with the rich, make this literature as useful as it can be, and lay the foundation for uniting humanity in a common intellectual conversation and quest for knowledge.[3]

The initiative recommended two complementary strategies to allow OA to peer-reviewed journal articles and unreviewed preprints—that scholars deposit their work in open electronic archives or institutional repositories, and that they transition to publishing in OA journals. These objectives were assisted at the time by the founding of the Open Archives Initiative (OAI), cited in the BOAI, which was established to develop and endorse technical interoperability standards for metadata catalogue information in archives and collections.[4]

Prompted by the OAI, e-print servers were introduced by university libraries in many parts of the world,[5] along with a growing number of OA journals, including the establishment of the OA publisher Public Library of Science (PLOS).[6] The BOAI called on researchers and their institutions to adopt next-generation forms of publishing to give all scholars, teachers, students, and engaged citizens free and unrestricted access to find, use, and share relevant literature available online for public benefit:

> An old tradition and a new technology have converged to make possible an unprecedented public good. The old tradition is the willingness of scientists and scholars to publish the fruits of their research in scholarly journals without payment, for the sake of inquiry and knowledge. The new technology is the internet.[7]

The BOAI's goals were reaffirmed on its tenth anniversary, and a new goal was added: that OA would become the default mode of "distributing new peer-reviewed research in every field and country" within the next decade.[8] On its twentieth anniversary in 2022, the BOAI's steering committee reflected on wider systemic challenges and the complexity of the OA ecosystem, making four high-level recommendations:

> 1. Host OA research on open infrastructure; 2. Reform research assessment and rewards to improve incentives; 3. Favor inclusive publishing and distribution channels that never exclude authors on economic grounds; and 4. When we spend money to publish OA research, remember the goals to which OA is the means.[9]

The authors emphasized the broader purpose: "OA is not an end in itself, but a means to other ends, above all, to the equity, quality, usability, and sustainability of research."[10]

A year after the original BOAI, the Bethesda Statement on Open Access Publishing principally focused on inspiring the biomedical community to adopt OA values and expediting the open sharing of primary scientific literature, noting, "This mission is only half-completed if the work is not made as widely available and as useful to society as possible."[11] It included sections on the roles of different stakeholders: institutions and funding agencies, libraries and publishers, and scientists and scientific societies. The statement identified the importance of faculty and researchers working closely with such organizations to develop a coordinated approach to publishing in OA journals and the need to recognize and reward adoption of OA principles when considering promotion, awards, and grants. It emphasized the "opportunity and the obligation" in sharing scientific research, pointing to the potential for education and outreach activities that mitigate inequity in access to research materials.[12]

The Berlin Declaration on Open Access to Knowledge in the Sciences and Humanities, also of 2003, intended to build on the BOAI and the Bethesda Statement. It reflected on the power of the internet "as an emerging functional medium for distributing knowledge":

> The Internet has fundamentally changed the practical and economic realities of distributing scientific knowledge and cultural heritage. For the first time ever, the Internet now offers the chance to constitute a global and interactive representation of human knowledge, including cultural heritage and the guarantee of worldwide access.[13]

The declaration represented a further concerted international call for OA, this time specifically including the humanities and focusing on issues for "research policy makers, research institutions, funding agencies, libraries, archives and museums."[14] It encouraged knowledge producers and cultural heritage holders to make their work more widely and readily available to society, maintain evaluation of OA contributions and online journals according to the highest standards of quality assurance, advocate for recognition and assessment of OA publishing in career progression and tenure, and further develop OA software, infrastructures, and tools.[15] Yet the declaration also recognized the challenges: "In order to realize the vision of a global and accessible representation of knowledge, the future Web has to be sustainable, interactive, and transparent. Content and software tools must be openly accessible and compatible."[16] Through ongoing annual meetings of its signatories and participants, the Berlin Declaration has continued to advocate its central principles and gain community backing.[17]

Collaboration for Greater Access

The BBB declarations were revolutionary in their time. Following these foundational statements, and with growing commitment to open approaches, international attention turned toward how best to foster collaborative exchanges to ensure the widest dissemination of not just research findings in the form of OA publications but also accompanying source materials, especially data. To this end, in 2004, the global nonprofit Open Knowledge Foundation (OKF) was established.[18] In the same year, the governments of thirty Organisation for Economic Co-operation and Development (OECD) countries—together with China, Israel, Russia, and South Africa—began work to develop a set of core Principles and Guidelines for Access to Research Data from Public Funding. Published in 2007, these principles and guidelines recognized that "access to research data increases the returns from public investment in this area; reinforces open scientific inquiry; encourages diversity of studies and opinion; promotes new areas of work and enables the exploration of topics not envisioned by the initial investigators."[19] The agreed-upon principles related to openness, flexibility, transparency, legal conformity, protection of intellectual property (IP), formal responsibility, professionalism, interoperability, quality, security, efficiency, accountability, and sustainability of access to research data. The Panton Principles for Open Data in Science in 2010 reinforced and further clarified these values.[20]

From the time of the OECD initiative, many significant statements have advocated greater equity in access to knowledge, through copyright revision and making available open educational resources (OERs) and open government data, and using alternative metrics and assessment approaches for responsive research and development. The 2005 Salvador Declaration on Open Access had highlighted that "Open Access promotes equity,"[21] envisaging outcomes commensurate with the UN Millennium Development Goals,[22] including large-scale collaborative partnerships for access to information, especially among developing countries. The 2007 Cape Town Open Education Declaration called for "a worldwide effort to make education both more accessible and more effective" by unlocking the potential of the "collaborative, interactive culture of the Internet," advocating for "the freedom to use, customize, improve and redistribute educational resources without constraint."[23] The 2011 Open Government Declaration—endorsed by seventy-eight participating nations calling for greater access to government information[24]—was followed by the 2014 Pisa Declaration to make gray literature (government, industry, and nongovernmental organization reports, working papers, documents, data, and other materials) more visible and accessible, recognizing "its importance for open access to research, open science, innovation, evidence-based policy, and knowledge transfer."[25]

All of these various policy frameworks and proclamations were, in addition to championing OA, aimed at achieving greater transparency, participation, and inclusive and accountable governance. The 2013 San Francisco Declaration on Research Assessment (DORA)[26] and the 2015 Leiden Manifesto for Research Metrics[27] recommended changes to universities' assessment criteria away from citation analysis–based metrics to social web usage analysis, observing levels of engagement and impact achieved via social media platforms, tools, and other online sharing activities. Many aspects of the wide-ranging statements discussed so far were brought together in the set of twelve Vienna Principles in 2016,[28] designed as a road map of key elements for the future of scholarly communication. These principles (set out in Table 2.1) illustrate core issues that frame current debates around open scholarship.

Accelerating the Transition to Open Scholarship

The notion of FAIR—findable, accessible, interoperable, and reusable was formulated at a Lorentz Workshop in 2014, which resulted in the FAIR Guiding Principles for Data Management and Stewardship published in 2016.[29] These FAIR principles have since become one of the most known expressions of the open scholarship movement. Expanding on conventional notions of what constitutes data, the FAIR principles are high-level values that cover "all digital scholarly research objects."[30] Recognizing the increasing volume and complexity of data, the emphasis is on managing, organizing, describing, and integrating data, and making data and metadata discoverable and reusable through it being not only "human-readable" but also "machine-actionable."[31] Rather than being a standard or specification, the FAIR principles precede any decisions on implementation or solutions. Governments and advocacy groups have been working to progressively refine and extend how the FAIR principles can best be implemented to maximize their value for increased public engagement. At

Table 2.1 The Vienna Principles: A Vision for Scholarly Communication

The Twelve Principles

1. Accessibility: *Scholarly communication should be immediately and openly accessible by anyone.*

The production of knowledge serves mankind and increases prosperity. Free and open dissemination of knowledge within the scientific community and beyond facilitates exchange, collaboration and the application of research results. There should be no technical, financial or legal obstacles delaying or preventing the accessibility of research findings. All research results should be accessible to people that are diverse in physical, economic and other conditions. Access should be ensured in the long-term.

2. Discoverability: *Scholarly communication should facilitate search, exploration and discovery.*

There have never been as many scholars as today, and never have they been as prolific as today due to new modes of communication and technology that is cheaper and more widely available. Researchers spend considerable time not only with communicating their own research, but also with staying up-to-date with the work of their colleagues. A system of scholarly communication should therefore organise scientific knowledge in such a way that it enables researchers and their stakeholders to efficiently and effectively identify research that is relevant to them. In addition, researchers should be able to find feedback on their own work and activities connected to it as easily as possible.

3. Reusability: *Scholarly communication should enable everyone to effectively build on top of each other's work.*

Following Newton's phrase "Standing on the shoulders of giants," modern scholarship is based on cooperation. Ideas are not created in a vacuum. Reuse of research processes, methods and results as well as abstraction and extension should therefore represent basic values of scholarly communication. The possibility to reuse data, materials and results enables researchers and communities to learn from each other and to speed up the production of new knowledge. Consequently, while appropriate attribution of authorship must be ensured, a maximum of reuse and processing should be permissible.

4. Reproducibility: *Scholarly communication should provide reproducible research results.*

Reproducibility of research findings is one of the distinctive features of research and a gold standard in many disciplines. As a minimum requirement, the research process should be traceable, e.g. by providing access to raw data and documenting the research process as well as the (intermediate) results (discussions, research diaries, pre-publications, etc.). This facilitates an understanding of the methodology and simplifies assessment. Opening up the methodology and production of results also helps to identify cases of unconscious wrongdoing, deception, and fraud. It should be possible to identify different stages of a research process and to understand its evolution.

The Twelve Principles

5. Transparency: *Scholarly communication should provide open and transparent means for judging the credibility of a research result.*

Virtually all new knowledge builds upon past findings, but in practice one cannot reproduce every research result to verify its credibility. A system of scholarly communication should therefore make it possible to judge the credibility of research results based on context information. This information may stem from the authors as well as from peer review or other forms of feedback. Context information should answer the five classic Ws: who, what, when, where and why, as well as the questions "Who paid for it?" and "How was it received?." Details on funding and on the relationship of researchers to study subjects highlight potential conflicts of interest and how ethical questions were addressed. Information that should be available at any point is whether a piece of research has been corrected or retracted after publication.

6. Understandability: *Scholarly communication should provide research in a clear, concise and understandable way adjusted to different stakeholders.*

A fruitful dialogue among researchers and between researchers and their stakeholders is mutually beneficial for both research and society. Keeping communication as clear and concise as possible facilitates knowledge transfer and exchange within research and beyond. What is considered clear and concise, however, is very dependent on the recipient and the situation. Communication amongst researchers usually involves a high degree of abstraction and special language, whereas communication with interested citizens requires more broadly understandable language. Scholarly communication should therefore be adapted for different stakeholder groups inside and outside of academia, by taking into account specific requirements in order to make it more meaningful and allowing for further involvement and participation.

7. Collaboration: *Scholarly communication should foster collaboration and participation between researchers and their stakeholders.*

Research is often of relevance to a great variety of stakeholders such as patients and doctors, students and teachers. Researchers and their stakeholders can benefit from working together, ranging from discussion over participation to real collaboration with lay communities in citizen science projects. Collaboration leads to a better understanding of research among stakeholders, and stakeholders can point out research questions that are important to them. Researchers can get feedback on their work, and in cases even receive support in conducting their research. Scholarly communication should therefore facilitate and encourage these forms of collaboration.

8. Quality Assurance: *Scholarly communication should provide transparent and competent review.*

Reviewing safeguards research discoveries, ensuring that results can be trusted and built upon. A system of scholarly communication should therefore incentivize, reward, and recognize reviewing, no less than doing research in order to create a balance between the production of knowledge and its consolidation. The primary function of reviewing should be to ensure that research is technically sound and that the results can be reproduced/that the research process is traceable. Transparent communication and open peer review can help to raise the quality of reviews and to avoid biased and hasty judgements.

(Continued)

Table 2.1 (*Continued*)

The Twelve Principles

9. Evaluation: *Scholarly communication should support fair evaluation.*

Evaluation influences the perceived impact of research results, researchers, journals or institutions, and therefore the way scientific knowledge is produced. It is therefore essential that these evaluation processes are conducted fairly and adequately. Assessment should offer an overall, multidimensional analysis, especially in an interdisciplinary context. Researchers should be given the opportunity to comment on evaluation results and they should be able to verify data collection and analysis processes. To build future research on solid ground, reward structures should be adopted and quality in research must be favoured over quantity. Adequate incentives should be provided to reward endeavours to publish better, rather than more.

10. Validated Progress: *Scholarly communication should promote both the production of new knowledge and the validation of existing knowledge.*

In order for scholarship to progress, it needs original research that contributes novel results to the body of knowledge. A system of scholarly communication should identify research gaps and highlight fields that need engagement and contribution. Uncertainty and risk-taking should be accepted in order to encourage testing of unusual methods and theories. But research also needs the validation of existing results in order to build future research on solid ground. Therefore, a system of scholarly communication should also promote the reproduction and continual validation of existing knowledge. The two functions should be appropriately balanced to achieve validated progress.

11. Innovation: *Scholarly communication should embrace the possibilities of new technology.*

Over the past 400 years, scholarly communication has been constantly evolving. This evolution has opened up new opportunities for researchers to work and collaborate. Therefore, scholarly communication should embrace the possibilities of new technology. The Web, in particular, has revolutionised the way we create, disseminate, explore and consume information, and its potentials are not fully exploited yet for scholarly communications. These potentials include real-time exchange and dissemination, ubiquitous and simultaneous availability of resources, zero marginal cost for dissemination, new workflows, improved reusability of data and results, the ability to process huge volumes of data and new forms of presenting and visualising results.

12. Public Good: *Scholarly communication should expand the knowledge commons.*

Scientific knowledge is critical for the development of society. As scientific knowledge is intangible in nature, its use by one person does not preclude its use by another person. On the contrary, knowledge tends to grow when it is shared. Therefore, no barriers should be established to restrict the use and reuse of research results. Scientific knowledge should be a public good and as such part of the knowledge commons, in order to enable everyone in society to benefit from this knowledge.

Source: Peter Kraker et al., "Vienna Principles: A Vision for Scholarly Communication," 2016, https://viennaprinciples.org/. Distributed under the terms of Creative Commons Attribution 4.0 International (CC BY 4.0).

the 2016 Group of Twenty (G20) Hangzhou summit, leaders issued a statement endorsing use of the FAIR principles aimed at promoting open science (OS), facilitating public access to research results, and fostering improved circulation of knowledge and education.[32] In the same year, the Amsterdam Call for Action on Open Science noted the potential to "increase the quality and benefits of science by making it faster, more responsive to societal challenges, more inclusive and more accessible to new users,"[33] and the European Commission unveiled its plans for the creation of the European Open Science Cloud (EOSC).[34]

In 2018, cOAlition S, a European consortium of major national agencies and funders from multiple countries, launched Plan S.[35] It called for all researchers who benefit from government-funded research to publish their work in OA journals or online platforms and to make data fully and immediately available through institutional repositories from 2021 onward.[36] These Plan S principles were reinforced in the São Paulo Statement on Open Access[37] and the Beijing Declaration on Research Data in 2019.[38] In response, many commercial publishers now have in place "transformative" agreements—also known as "transitional" and including "read and publish" or "publish and read" agreements—with institutions (universities, libraries, and regional consortia) that allow a transition period from subscription licensing to OA, via a range of inclusions that varies according to negotiated contracts.[39] Universities, primarily in developed countries, are entering into one-on-one agreements and membership programs with major publishers, involving reduced OA embargo periods, discounts on subscription fees and article processing charges (APCs) or book processing charges (BPCs), and other options.[40] Transformative agreements are aimed at fostering equity in publishing and ensuring that author needs and those of their institutions are addressed.

Lacking the resources of other major blocs, Latin America has adopted a different approach focused on scholarly communication networks outside the commercial publishing system, enabling academics to publish and share their research free of charge while also allowing broader public access.[41] For example, SciELO (Scientific Electronic Library Online) is a database, library, and OA publishing model aimed at increasing visibility and access to research literature for developing countries. Established in Brazil in 1997, it now provides a portal for accessing journals and publications from fifteen Latin American countries, as well as South Africa. Redalyc (Red de Revistas Científicas de América Latina, y El Caribe, España y Portugal) is a similar service aimed at building a scientific information system made up of leading journals, edited in Latin America and Iberia, representing multiple disciplines.[42] AmeliCA (Open Knowledge

Non-profit Academy-Owned Open Access, formerly Open Knowledge for Latin America and the Global South) is an aligned communication infrastructure for scholarly publishing and OS.[43] LA Referencia (the Federated Network of Institutional Repositories of Scientific Publications) is supported by countries whose open repositories follow interoperability standards.[44] Importantly, Latin American universities encourage staff to use these networks and repositories rather than paying APCs or BPCs.[45]

It has been UNESCO's commitment that has arguably most influenced and broadened the concept of openness in terms of "pluralistic knowledge societies"[46] that are "inclusive, equitable, open and participatory,"[47] aiming at more equal access for global public good:

> By Knowledge Societies, UNESCO means societies in which people have the capabilities not just to acquire information but also to transform it into knowledge and understanding, which empowers them to enhance their livelihoods and contribute to the social and economic development of their societies.[48]

In this context, UNESCO has emphasized increasing availability, dissemination, and preservation of information with a vision that extends far beyond access issues to underscore the value of shared knowledge for mutual understanding and respect:

> Access to knowledge through education and science allows us to develop and share our values, for the development of humanity. It allows individuals to improve their quality of life. This quality of life is the basis for individual peace, and individual peace is the basis for collective peace.[49]

UNESCO has more recently formulated a strategy on Open Access to Scientific Research—including the 2017 UNESCO Recommendation on Science and Scientific Researchers[50] and a 2019 Recommendation on Open Educational Resources[51]—among other activities, including the Global Open Access Portal,[52] which highlights OA events, mandates, and publications in countries worldwide.

The UNESCO Recommendation on Open Science,[53] adopted in November 2021, expands on these initiatives (see Table 2.2 for a summary of historical events in scholarly communication, including, most recently, this recommendation). In 2019, at the fortieth session of UNESCO's General Conference, 193 member states launched a global consultation process with the goal of formulating a coherent vision of OS and a set of overarching principles and shared values.

The resultant recommendation centers on the development of an international framework aimed at creating a culture of openness at all levels. Its key objectives and areas of action are as follows:

  i. promoting a common understanding of open science, associated benefits and challenges, as well as diverse paths to open science;
 ii. developing an enabling policy environment for open science;
iii. investing in open science infrastructures and services;
 iv. investing in human resources, training, education, digital literacy and capacity building for open science;
  v. fostering a culture of open science and aligning incentives for open science;
 vi. promoting innovative approaches for open science at different stages of the scientific process;
vii. promoting international and multi-stakeholder cooperation in the context of open science and with view to reducing digital, technological and knowledge gaps.[54]

Released against the backdrop of the Covid-19 health crisis, the recommendation notes the impact of the pandemic on research practices and the need for rapid information and data sharing. Covid-19

> has proven worldwide the urgency of and need for fostering equitable access to scientific information, facilitating the sharing of scientific knowledge, data and information, enhancing scientific collaboration and science- and knowledge-based decision making to respond to global emergencies and increase the resilience of societies.[55]

The recommendation builds on four key pillars: "open scientific knowledge, open science infrastructures, open engagement of societal actors, and open dialogue with other knowledge systems."[56] The open scientific knowledge component is supported by scientific publications, open research data, open educational resources, open source software and source code, and open hardware. The infrastructural component may be physical or virtual, responding to the needs of different research communities. In the case of the open engagement component, various modes of interaction might include crowdfunding, crowdsourcing, scientific volunteering, and citizen and participatory science. The open dialogue component is linked with encouraging engagement with Indigenous peoples, marginalized scholars, and local communities. Values and principles set out in the recommendation underline fairness, diversity, inclusiveness, equality of opportunity, collaboration and sustainability, and others, with the aim of addressing existing systemic inequities and guiding scientific work in solving

Table 2.2 Key Events Influencing Scholarly Communication

3400–3100 BCE	The earliest known forms of writing come from the ancient city of Uruk, in southern Mesopotamia (modern Iraq), where the script of the Sumerian language began to develop on clay tablets, followed shortly by Egyptian hieroglyphics.
Seventh century BCE	The Assyrian king Ashurbanipal systematically amassed a significant collection of cuneiform texts on clay and wooden tablets as his personal library and for imperial purposes.
c.300 BCE	The Great Library of Alexandria, one of the largest of the ancient world, was established as a center for learning to preserve and store a broad repository of knowledge from many societies; it is known to have contained vast collections of papyrus rolls and also pioneered alphabetical ordering of its holdings.
c.197–c.159 BCE	The Library of Pergamum (in present-day Turkey) was founded. This library housed manuscripts written on parchment, which was established as a thriving local industry.
206 BCE–9 CE	The imperial collection of the Former Han dynasty, often described as the first Chinese library, is the earliest known to have a catalog, ordered chronologically and by category for reference.
1323	Learned societies began to emerge in Europe, bringing together scholars with similar interests to exchange and debate ideas and concepts. The oldest of these was Compagnie du Gai Sçavoir founded in Toulouse, France.
c.1450	Gutenberg's printing press introduced movable type, which had originated in China, to Europe. This allowed multiple copies of a work to be produced, distributed, and shared more easily, increasing the circulation of knowledge.
1454	The Malatestiana Library in Cesena, Italy, opened. Known to have been the first civic library in Europe to make both secular and religious texts fully open to the public, it is the world's oldest extant public library.
1665	The *Journal des Sçavans* and *Philosophical Transactions* were the first academic journals, established by learned societies for scholarly communication and review of new knowledge by members through letter-excerpts, summaries of recently published books, and accounts of observations and experiments.
1710	England introduced the Statute of Anne, the first modern copyright law, granting authors of books, journals, and other writings the sole right to decide and consent to whether and by whom their work could be printed, reprinted, or published, with the aim of promoting learning and curtailing the copying and claiming of credit for original work.

c.1700–c.1800	During the Enlightenment, with its ideals of liberty, reason, and scientific progress, the establishment of learned societies continued, and there was a growth in periodicals, which numbered in the hundreds by the end of the eighteenth century. Literacy rates rose significantly in Europe, resulting in wider sharing of knowledge.
1806	Henry Fourdrinier's invention of a continuous papermaking machine in the era of industrialization made it relatively inexpensive to produce large quantities of publications at high speed.
1927	The journal *Science* published a paper regarded as the first to use citation counts as an indicator of the significance of scientific research.
1939–1945	During the Second World War, governments around the world, particularly the United States, invested significantly in university research and the professionalization of the research community.
1945	Vannevar Bush supported the concept of academics being left to freely direct their own research agendas to solve societal problems. This set the scene for academic boards dominated by elite scholars to judge research excellence, with publications becoming the principal means of assessing academic performance globally.
1951	Entrepreneur Robert Maxwell bought the company he renamed Pergamon Press, developing it into a highly profitable commercial venture. He became aware that academics not only write and peer-review publications and serve on editorial boards free of charge, but their university libraries also would be willing to pay subscription fees.
1964	With the growth in the number of academic journals, Eugene Garfield developed a system to rank journals according to a citation-based metric, or the impact factor, as a way of assessing quality.
1970s	The "serial pricing crisis" began as large commercial publishers increased their prices exponentially for high-impact journals, outstripping libraries' financial and administrative capacities.
1970s–1980s	Ongoing development of computer networks and digital infrastructure, including the creation of shared protocols and standards for how data could be sent and received, led to the establishment of the internet.
1983	The free software movement was launched to promote sharing of source code by programmers and users, pioneering the concept of "copyleft" (building on the term *copyright*) and leading to the first general public licenses to preserve the legal right to use, study, modify, and redistribute software free of charge and without restriction.

(*Continued*)

Table 2.2 (*Continued*)

1991	The World Wide Web was introduced to the general public, revolutionizing society by providing users with ready access to vast amounts of online information.
1991	arXiv.com was developed as a preprint server to make research literature freely available online.
1993	The World Wide Web was put into the public domain as an open standard by the European Organization for Nuclear Research (CERN).
1997	SciELO (Scientific Electronic Library Online)—a bibliographic database, digital library, and cooperative electronic publishing model of OA journals—was established in Brazil to meet the scholarly communication needs of developing countries and to provide an efficient way to increase visibility and access to academic literature.
1998	The Scholarly Publishing and Academic Resources Coalition (SPARC), an alliance of academic libraries and other organizations, was established to seek more accessible alternatives to the commercial publishers' high-price subscription model for scholarly publications.
Late 1990s–Early 2000s	Publishers introduced "big deal" subscriptions to their serial journals, with some abandoning the sale of journals and books in favor of libraries purchasing online access rather than ownership, but as prices continued to surge, the socioeconomic, cultural, and digital divide grew between universities in the Global North and South.
2001	The Creative Commons nonprofit organization was established to develop licenses giving authors the right to share their work more freely with the general public.
2002–2003	The Budapest Open Access Initiative, the Bethesda Statement on Open Access Publishing, and the Berlin Declaration on Access to Knowledge in the Sciences and Humanities (BBB) called for international standards to promote free access to all academic articles for the use, reuse, modification, and redistribution of research findings and literature.
Early 2000s	University-based institutional repositories were set up as services committed to collection, classification, curation, preservation, and provision of OA to their research outputs.
Early 2000s	The article processing charge (APC) and book processing charge (BPC) were introduced as a cost levied to authors by many publishers in order to make their publications freely available online.
2003	The Directory of Open Access Journals (DOAJ) was established as an index to OA journals, aiming at increasing the global visibility of OA scholarly research publishers.

2004	The Open Knowledge Foundation (OKF), a global nonprofit network, was launched to promote openness in the creation of, access to, and dissemination of all forms of knowledge.
2005	The *h*-index was developed to rank authors based on their publication activity and citation levels.
2006	The highly ranked not-for-profit OA mega-journal *PLOS ONE* was established.
c.2004–2008	Academia.edu, Google Scholar, Mendeley, ResearchGate, and other social networking sites emerged, providing researchers with a way to manage, share, and find research papers and potential collaborators.
2005–2008	The Research Councils of the United Kingdom, the Canadian Institutes of Health Research, and the US National Institutes of Health introduced various OA mandates (e.g., for deposit of research materials in e-print or institutional repositories, or for research papers resulting from government funding to be made freely and publicly available within a certain time frame of publication). This was followed by similar mandates by the European Research Council.
2010	The Altmetrics Manifesto introduced new measures for assessing the impact of scholarly research based on social web analytics.
2012	The San Francisco Declaration on Research Assessment (DORA), which recognized the need to improve ways in which research and scholarly outputs are evaluated, was developed.
2012	Several innovative journals, including *F1000Research*, *PeerJ*, and *eLife*, were launched, experimenting with new forms of peer review, online access, and business models including new revenue sources.
2015	The Open Research Funders Group (ORFG) was established with the support of major funding bodies and SPARC to develop principles and practical solutions to accelerate OA and data policy.
2016	The FAIR Guiding Principles for Data Management and Stewardship were published. At the G20 Hangzhou summit, leaders issued a statement endorsing the application of these principles, which were later mandated in numerous international organizations and have become one of the most known expressions of the open scholarship movement.
2018	cOAlition S, a European and international consortium of research funders and organizations, launched Plan S, requiring that from 2021 all publications that result from publicly funded research grants must be published via OA journals or platforms.
2021	The UNESCO Recommendation on Open Science was adopted to address current barriers to open scholarship and to forge opportunities for a workable, equitable, and sustainable path for improving openness in all research.

the most significant human challenges. This ambitious and forward-looking framework represents an important step toward, and plan for, realizing the vision of connected open scholarship.

National Government and Funding Agency Mandates

Many national research councils have been calling for the widest possible dissemination of outputs arising from government-funded projects and for these to be deposited into OA institutional repositories as soon as practicable. Since 2005, the Research Councils of the United Kingdom have required deposit of funded research into an e-print repository where available.[57] The Canadian Institutes of Health Research included the responsibility to deposit research in institutional repositories in 2007, later leading to the Tri-Agency Open Access Policy on Publications in 2015. The US National Institutes of Health introduced an OA mandate in 2008 requiring that research papers be made freely and publicly available within twelve months of publication. This was followed by similar mandates from the European Research Council, with OA to the findings of all European Commission–funded research required from 2014.[58] As noted, Plan S specified that, from 2021, all academic publications resulting from publicly funded grants be published through compliant OA journals or platforms. Under these and other guidelines, academics must ensure that anyone can obtain free access to the full text of government-funded research outputs at any time. Governments are also expanding these policies to include OA not only to research literature but also to data.[59] At the individual researcher level, the nonprofit ORCID (Open Researcher and Contributor ID)[60] is being widely used and often is now required by government agencies to verify researcher identity and register trusted information about research outputs.

In addition to universities and research entities having their own individual institutional repositories, there is a strong case for the linking of these repositories. While there are successful examples of institutional, national, and regional platforms, there is no global interoperability framework for institutional repositories. Associations of repositories, such as the Confederation of Open Access Repositories (COAR), advocate for the connecting of separate repositories to form networks to build capacity, align policies and practice, and work toward a global ecosystem. As COAR states in its manifesto, "Each individual repository is of limited value for research: the real power of Open Access lies in the possibility of connecting and tying together repositories, which is why we need interoperability."[61] Achieving this linkage requires further investment in coordinated infrastructure. Open Access Infrastructure for Research in Europe (OpenAIRE) is one example that, with the assistance of the European Commission, has formed a large network of OA repositories and services embedded in national infrastructures.[62]

An increasing number of philanthropic organizations are pledging support for open scholarship. Change is being driven via the Open Research Funders Group (ORFG), a partnership of philanthropic organizations dedicated to open sharing, including developing practical solutions for monitoring OA and open data policy compliance and tracking impact. The Open Research Funders Group currently includes, among others, the Alfred P. Sloan Foundation, the Bill and Melinda Gates Foundation, the Open Society Foundations, and the Robert Wood Johnson Foundation. Libraries also continue to play a central role in the campaign for OA through the pursuit of practical solutions for disseminating research, including through library associations such as the International Federation of Library Associations and Institutions (IFLA), SciELO, Ligue des Bibliothèques Européennes de Recherche—Association of European Research Libraries (LIBER), Electronic Information for Libraries (EIFL), and many more.

As the open scholarship movement goes forward and further mandates are implemented, commitment to the philosophies, values, and principles of openness is growing.[63] Yet, as the following chapter outlines, fundamental challenges need addressing across all parts of the system and at various levels, from individual and institutional to national and global.

3

Barriers in Implementing Open Scholarship

For more than two decades, the open scholarship movement has experienced positive momentum and sustained commitment, energy, and goodwill toward the establishment of clear charters and calls for action. However, it has also faced challenges. This chapter reviews the implementation of open practices in different contexts by investigating multiple stakeholder perspectives and roles, from the international to the institutional and individual levels. These include those of government and philanthropic funding agencies, policymakers and peak bodies, publishers, senior university administrators, researchers, librarians, students, information and communications technology (ICT) specialists and platform developers, as well as the broader community. The discussion identifies socioeconomic, cultural, institutional, operational, attitudinal, technical, legal, and resource-level obstacles, and how these might be overcome through effective communication and collaboration between all tiers of participants.

Socioeconomic, Cultural, and Equity Divides

At the heart of open scholarship is the drive for greater equity of access to and engagement with research and education to bridge digital divides.[1] From the outset, the movement has sought to make trusted digital resources available globally, representing a concerted drive toward democratization of access to the results of research. There is immense potential for digital communication channels to assist in building and supporting sustainable "knowledge societies," yet at the macro level the opportunities are unequally distributed.[2] Limited internet access, coverage, stability, and affordability; low user ability or digital literacy; and crucially the cost of making research openly available are basic barriers to online participation that can reinforce global North-South imbalances and related inequalities within and across borders.[3] The challenges are amplified where filtering or censorship restrictions are imposed and when language barriers exist.

A key focus of open scholarship has been on improving information access in developing countries.[4] Very large portions of the global population remain without access to the internet or are missing the infrastructure, tools, or skills to benefit in meaningful or affordable ways. Many citizens, consequently, have been almost completely shut out from the digital revolution and its benefits. Inclusion, diversity, and justice need to guide development of the global open scholarly ecosystem. As the United Nations Declaration of Human Rights states, "Everyone has the right to freely participate in the cultural life of the community, to enjoy the arts and to share in scientific advancement and its benefits."[5]

Digital divides can occur along socioeconomic, geographic, ethnic, class, gender, age, and other lines, and so openness does not straightforwardly correlate with inclusion. Minority and Indigenous populations are shown to have lower digital inclusion.[6] By various measures, more than 50 percent of all academic literature is published by the five biggest companies: Elsevier, Sage, Springer, Taylor and Francis, and Wiley-Blackwell.[7] Distribution of open access (OA) research outputs is dominated by North American and European publishers and platforms that tend to privilege networks of established authors and reinforce the dominance of English.[8] Far fewer OA publications originate in African, Asian, and Central and South American countries, and in languages other than English. Being unable to participate in big-deal publisher packages—unaffordable for large parts of the world—has significant implications for equity. This can also inadvertently legitimize illegal file sharing and copyright violation.[9] Similar issues apply to data. The cost associated with collecting high-quality data curtails research in many countries. Making data openly available, using standardized formats so they can be readily retrieved and reused, reduces costs and duplication.[10]

Institutional and Policy Barriers

University leaders—senior administrators, faculty deans, professors, and directors of research centers and programs—are increasingly being required to commit to change in the academic culture and implement long-term plans for a more open and engaged research environment. However, coordinating this shift across the multiple levels of the university system is a complex task, involving a wide range of internal and external drivers and stakeholders.[11] Lack of incentives, recognition, and training for the open sharing of research is a key challenge.[12]

Faculty and research leaders are in an influential position to build bridges between senior university administrators, academics, students, and the broader community through research, teaching, and service, and by promoting university policy, yet institutional backing is often inadequate.[13] Further challenges confronting these leaders may include general lack of staff awareness or clear understanding of the merits of open scholarship, scarcity of funds to train academics and students in the use of new tools and to support the development and maintenance of relevant digital resources, and lack of familiarity with legal agreements and software licenses.[14] Universities need to actively encourage the use of institutional repositories and platforms for OA to data, software, and other digital assets, in addition to academic publications. While many do offer staff training on OA and data management, these are generally one-off introductory activities and do not involve researchers in ongoing hands-on learning through real-world application of skills.[15] Insufficient training leaves academics, particularly early-career researchers, with little opportunity to develop open scholarship strategies.[16]

Arguably, the key institutional barrier to implementing open practices is that academic performance continues to be judged and funded according to a merit system and world rankings regime based primarily on evaluating research achievements according to traditional publication and citation metrics (see Chapter 5).[17] Considered together, the factors discussed here are impeding a system-wide understanding and step change needed for institutions to enable greater engagement and openness.[18] Universities can take a leading role by recognizing the proactive stance they might adopt in addressing these many institutional and policy barriers.

Technological and Operational Obstacles

University librarians can be major advocates for implementing open practices— educating staff about the benefits of OA journals and platforms; giving advice on alternative publishing mechanisms and copyright to help researchers make their outputs more available; providing information on access, citations, and impact to promote positive attitudes; offering technical support to improve discoverability through optimizing descriptive metadata; and assisting with data preservation and security.[19]

At the operational level, barriers confronted by librarians and ICT staff include lack of time, opportunities, and resources to advocate for the benefits of self-archiving and data sharing via institutional repositories; inadequate provision of newer-generation software and infrastructure to facilitate easy deposit, storage, and retrieval; shortage of funding for ongoing management, safeguarding, and migration of data;[20] limited institutional guidelines around preferred formats and licensing requirements to present research data in more findable, accessible, interoperable, and reusable (FAIR) ways; and low levels of staff training to encourage the uptake of OA and open scholarship—all of which can cause frustration and reduce motivation.[21] These barriers can be compounded in cases where there are hosting arrangements with external organizations.[22] While university institutional repositories are pivotal for the creation of a more dynamic approach to open scholarship, they can be siloed.[23] Working closely with ICT staff and platform providers, senior librarians and university administrators can plan and design more open infrastructure. As noted, there are calls for greater collaboration to connect standalone repositories into larger networks. With the range of software and repository solutions expanding, there is a need for sector-wide protocols and standards to ensure ideal functionality and interoperability of systems.[24]

Financial and Legal Factors

The open scholarship movement has focused on unrestricted "free" access to enhance scholarly communication. Yet providing OA to research publications can involve costly processing charges, representing a "financial elitism" that goes against principles of openness.[25] While universities may offer monetary assistance for gold OA, when this is available it tends to be provided to researchers publishing in top-tier journals—once again placing emphasis on traditional standards and favoring the large international publishers. It is reasonable to ask why budgets for research should have to incorporate article processing charges (APCs) or book processing charges (BPCs) for OA publishing when research outputs could be made freely and immediately available via alternative means. Many institutions are lobbying for change as mandates are being introduced that require researchers to place their work in OA venues.

Making scholarly information more widely available in digital formats has, however, also raised complex questions relating to intellectual property infringement and copyright laws. Libraries, universities, and regulatory bodies have a responsibility to oversee and monitor use and reproduction of materials to guard against copyright infringement. Whereas publications almost always attract copyright protection, ensuring that data are protected and able to be shared is more complicated, as copyright does not generally apply to data.[26] There has always been a balance to be struck between affording authors tighter control of their work and giving the broader public permission to distribute, reuse, and expand on this work. Changes to copyright regulations in many countries have been made to navigate these pressures,[27] yet knowing when a work falls into the public domain and how it can be used can still be difficult.[28]

The barriers discussed so far show complexity at all levels in achieving open scholarship. Table 3.1 provides a summary of the kinds of barriers faced. While the list is extensive, the identification of as many barriers as possible is a necessary step toward addressing those that may apply in specific contexts with a view to managing or overcoming them.

Overcoming Barriers

Successful implementation of open initiatives depends on building a commitment to the philosophies of openness and broadening opportunities for more productive and readily available public access to knowledge.[29] This requires changes in approach across government agencies, funders, university administration, libraries, the research community, and the ICT industry. Table 3.2 illustrates the roles that key stakeholders can play in this process. It focuses on positive strategies, approaches, and support that can facilitate the wider adoption and application of open scholarship principles. Individual researchers work within universities and institutes that are funded by government agencies, philanthropic entities, and industry groups. Their research is supported through libraries, scholarly communication societies, other universities, participants from the general public, and—of particular relevance to the humanities—by cultural and collecting institutions, including galleries, libraries, archives, and museums (GLAM).[30] Ultimately, their research materials are presented and shared through academic and commercial publishers, open knowledge groups and platforms, editors, journalists, institutional repositories, and via ICT. The motives for making research openly available may vary significantly among stakeholders, and yet there is a clear and urgent need for shared vision to create a more collaborative and open environment.

Chapter 4 considers the issues raised in this and earlier chapters through the lens of the humanities, including the challenges posed by diverse forms of research outputs and data.

Table 3.1 Barriers to Open Scholarship

Socioeconomic, cultural, and equity	• Limited coverage, stability, and affordability impedes access to the internet for a large portion of the global population. • Low digital literacy hinders online participation and contributes to the digital divide. • The overall costs involved in making research openly available can be prohibitive. • Where filtering or censorship restrictions are imposed, the barriers to digital inclusion are intensified. • Issues of privacy and cultural sensitivity can present complex challenges. • The lack of infrastructure, tools, or skills to participate in the digital environment further exacerbates socioeconomic, geographic, cultural, gender, and other forms of inequality and exclusion within and across borders. • North American and European publishers and platforms dominate the distribution of OA research outputs, reinforcing global North-South divides. • Open access journals produced by international publishers reinforce overrepresentation of dominant primary language groups (English; also Mandarin, Spanish, and Arabic). • The fees for big-deal publisher packages render them unaffordable for much of the world. • The expense of collecting high-quality data inhibits research in many countries.
Institutional and policy	• There is a lack of incentives, recognition, and training for the open sharing of research. • Faculty and research leaders often do not have clearly articulated institutional backing to promote open approaches. • Limited staff awareness or understanding of the merits of open scholarship slows implementation and uptake. • The culture of "publish or perish" limits development of new forms of open scholarship and engagement. • The perception of lack of prestige continues for many OA journals. • Open scholarship is given low priority in the face of competing demands relating to maintaining high productivity levels, including funding applications, administration, teaching, and other duties. • University ranking systems continue to focus on scholarly publication and citation analysis rather than on the sharing of knowledge through open platforms and repositories. • There is a lack of global agreement and guidelines to fully implement open scholarship policies, which vary from country to country.

Technical and operational	• Librarians and ICT staff need time, opportunities, and resources to advocate for the benefits of self-archiving and data sharing via institutional repositories. • There is an ongoing need for software and infrastructure upgrades. • Funding is required for ICT services, infrastructure, and data management, migration, and preservation. • Clear institutional guidelines are required for preferred formats and licensing requirements to present research data in more FAIR ways. • Staff professional development is needed to encourage the uptake of OA and scholarship. • Sector-wide protocols and standards are required to foster and support interoperability of institutional repositories.
Financial and legal	• There is a scarcity of funding for open resources and practices. • Costly APCs and/or BPCs continue to primarily benefit large international publishers. • Lengthy embargo periods exist to protect publisher revenues. • There is a risk of open scholarship practices infringing intellectual property and copyright laws. • Ensuring data are protected can be complex, as copyright does not apply to data. • No widely agreed-upon large-scale solutions are available for providing cost-effective OA for books.

Table 3.2 The Role of Stakeholders in Promoting Open Practices

Stakeholder Groups	Key Roles
Researchers	Researchers are the main producers and users of research outputs and data, and they can actively collaborate with all stakeholders so that results are made available in formats that are easily discoverable, usable, understandable, and preservable to ensure accuracy and quality, and for reuse. They are most likely to engage in open research if they are actively supported, that is, if the academic environment incentivizes, recognizes, and rewards open scholarship; provides infrastructure, training, and time; offers financial assistance to cover the costs of making publications openly accessible; and delivers data management services and platforms for storing and sharing research outputs.
Universities and research institutions	Universities and research institutions can work together with scholarly societies, funding agencies, publishers, and the ICT industry to emphasize the importance of open approaches that cater to researchers. There is a need to establish agreed-upon standards and develop university ranking systems that encourage public engagement and benefit rather than remaining focused on traditional bibliometric indicators.

(*Continued*)

Table 3.2 (*Continued*)

Stakeholder Groups	Key Roles
Libraries and institutional repositories	Librarians can be key advocates for open scholarship, supporting researchers to make outputs and data more openly available. Institutional repositories enable research to be more discoverable, accessible, reusable, transparent, and sustainable (DARTS).
Academic and commercial publishers	Publishers facilitate scholarly communication and can play a crucial role by adapting their publishing policies to support OA and by using Creative Commons licensing to ensure that academic publications reach a wider readership.
Journal editors	Journal editors can play a significant role in promoting open practices. Through communicating the benefits of OA publishing to the academic community (including authors, peer reviewers, and editorial boards), journal editors can take a leadership role in helping to transform the publishing landscape.
Collecting institutions/ GLAM sector	Collecting institutions are custodians of some of the most significant source materials for research in many disciplines, especially in the humanities. The GLAM sector can proactively expand OA to content and data for research purposes and for the preservation of cultural heritage.
Public and private funding agencies	In addition to mandating that all publications resulting from funded research should be published via OA journals or platforms, public and private funding agencies can promote optimal use and reuse of data, and they can play a central role in raising awareness of the importance of sound data management practices.
ICT industry and infrastructure groups	ICT technicians and system designers can support university librarians and senior administrators and can plan and provision institutional infrastructure to be as open and interoperable as possible.
Global or regional entities and initiatives	Global entities, such as the United Nations Educational, Scientific and Cultural Organization (UNESCO), can promote international policy directives and open research initiatives, and in so doing help in gaining the support of governments and major funding agencies. Regional initiatives can foster awareness, education, and uptake at the local level.
Engaged citizens	Engaged citizens can play an active role in enabling open scholarship through increased participation and engagement including via crowdsourcing; assisting in collection, curation, and transcription; gathering new ideas; and helping solve problems through open collaboration.

4

Toward the Open Humanities

This chapter explores a wide range of issues and opportunities relating to open scholarship in the humanities, arguing that there is a need to develop a stronger framework in which to enable open humanities rather than simply reapplying approaches drawn from open science. While the humanities and sciences share a common commitment to many of the core principles driving the open scholarship movement, aspects of scholarship in the humanities have different aims, purposes, and methodologies from those of the sciences, so they may be enabled or supported differently by openness, in response to the varied disciplinary contexts and research workflows relevant to knowledge production and sharing in this broad domain. The discussion begins by reviewing significant differences between the humanities and sciences in approach and outputs before focusing on humanities open access publishing and emerging publication formats, data sharing, the development of research infrastructure, and social and community-based forms of knowledge creation.

Open Science or Open Humanities?

Discourse on open scholarship, as noted through this book, has, to date, centered predominantly on *open science* (OS)—a term first used in relation to the sciences[1] but now often extended to cover all disciplines, including those of the humanities:

> Open science (OS) comprises a set of institutional policies, infrastructure and relationships related to open access publication, open data and scientific resources, and lack of restrictive intellectual and other proprietary rights with the goal of increasing the quality and credibility of scientific outputs, increasing efficiency, and spurring both discovery and innovation.[2]

Broadly, open scholarship, across the sciences or humanities, enables increased access to knowledge, facilitates the sharing of scholarship through collaborative networks, and improves research standards through greater accuracy, integrity, accountability, replicability, and generalizability.[3] However, the use of the umbrella term *open science* to cover all disciplines itself plays a role in prioritizing the sciences over the humanities in the context of open scholarship.

The United Nations Educational, Scientific and Cultural Organization (UNESCO) Recommendation on Open Science defines OS in a way that includes the humanities and also highlights multilingualism:

> Open science is defined as an inclusive construct that combines various movements and practices aiming to make multilingual scientific knowledge openly available, accessible and reusable for everyone, to increase scientific collaborations and sharing of information for the benefits of science and society, and to open the processes of scientific knowledge creation, evaluation and communication to societal actors beyond the traditional scientific community. It comprises all scientific disciplines and aspects of scholarly practices, including basic and applied sciences, natural and social sciences and the humanities, and it builds on the following key pillars: open scientific knowledge, open science infrastructures, science communication, open engagement of societal actors and open dialogue with other knowledge systems.[4]

The above definitions of OS align with the whole-of-ecosystem approach to open scholarship, which, as discussed, aims to enable researchers, policymakers, industry, and engaged citizens to draw from, borrow, repurpose, and build on already developed research outputs, methods, and data. They not only align with the mandate of open scholarship to disseminate knowledge but also allow for reviewing and checking of study designs, data, and analysis when these are made openly available.[5]

While definitions of OS and accompanying policies have increasingly sought to include all disciplines rather than having a bias toward the sciences, the reality remains that the requirements of the humanities are not as often taken into consideration as those of the sciences. Compared with science, technology, engineering, and mathematics (STEM) fields, the humanities have been relatively slow to engage with and take advantage of the open scholarship movement—for many reasons.[6] While development of the Budapest Open Access Initiative, Bethesda Statement, and Berlin Declaration (BBB) involved representatives from the humanities, the principal drivers of open access (OA) and open scholarship policies had their origins in the sciences, with the humanities very much on the sideline.⁷

Strong arguments can be made for considering the particular issues and needs of the humanities separately and advocating for *open humanities* as a key area of open scholarship. Although many aspects of open humanities necessarily need to follow the approaches and standards developed in OS and the broader open scholarship movement, there are also opportunities for the humanities to develop their own frameworks for openness and to participate in and reap the benefits of open scholarship on a much larger scale than is currently the case. According to an early working definition over a decade ago, "the open humanities are those aspects of the humanities aimed at democratizing production and consumption of humanities research."⁸ Yet beyond having very different publishing practices, discussed in the next section, other notable differences set the humanities apart and require separate consideration. These differences relate not only to applications of openness but also, more fundamentally, to the epistemologies and histories of the humanities and sciences. Representing two very distinct realms of research and work, they have often been referred to as the *two cultures*, the term C. P. Snow used in his influential Rede Lecture of 1959, which continues to apply.⁹

In policy and practical discussions of open scholarship, there has tended to be little consideration of substantial differences between the epistemologies underlying the humanities and sciences. Scientific methods supported by positivism start with a tightly defined theory from which a hypothesis can be deducted, tested, verified, replicated, and generalized to represent a broader group of phenomena.¹⁰ Scientific research often sets out from the starting point of a hypothesis to be proved or disproved. The theoretical assumption around positivism is that research should be objective, tangible, and governed by universal and rational laws—employing, for example, random sampling, high levels of measurement, and reductive data analysis to explain, predict, and discover causes and consequences.¹¹ Research in the humanities, by contrast, centers on interpretivism and critical analysis to explore how social worlds are constructed, interpreted, and assigned meaning, and how they may be shaped by conflicts, tensions, and contradictions that could influence individual and social behaviors and beliefs—and change over time.¹² Humanities scholars thus tend to use inductive approaches to gain a deeper consideration and subjective interpretation of reality as people see it to be, rather than seeking the objectivity of the sciences that is focused on the goal of unbiased, systematic, and logical outputs that separate facts from values. In the humanities, personal interpretation and values-based critical analysis are important dimensions of scholarly investigation.[13] Operating in nonlinear and nonuniform ways, the philosophies underlying the humanities are likely to be dependent on a culture of debate to generate questions and engage with a variety of methods of analysis through, for example, source criticism, hermeneutics, nuance, contextual meaning, and phenomenology. These encourage rational exchange and communication for deeper understanding and knowledge production but do not necessarily seek answers or closure.[14]

While such generalizations about cultural differences between science and humanities disciplines necessarily represent major simplifications, especially since so many disciplines fall under each of those headings, differences between the two realms can be identified and need to be acknowledged in order to focus attention on the humanities as something other than a subcategory of science. Within a discussion on the functioning of disciplines, Michel Foucault writes,

> In reality, the disciplines have their own discourse. They engender ... apparatuses of knowledge (*savoir*) and a multiplicity of new domains of understanding. ... [At] the advance front of the exact sciences the uncertain, recalcitrant, confused dominion of human behaviour has little by little been annexed to science.[15]

After six decades, C. P. Snow's analysis still has relevance: "The reasons for the existence of the two cultures are many, deep, and complex, some rooted in social histories, some in personal histories, and some in the inner dynamic of the different kinds of mental activity themselves."[16] The humanities tend to place more emphasis than the sciences on open-ended exploration, experimentation, cultural context, theoretical critique, and human emotion. These characteristics influence the ways and extent to which scholarship can be made openly available. Such basic differences in approach also have flow-on effects for developing open solutions. There are, for example, differences in workflow that separate the humanities and sciences and have a bearing on how the results of research can be made open. The sciences place emphasis on transparency, replicability, reusability, and, in some contexts, industrial applicability, principles that are not readily transferred into the humanities or have a different meaning there.[17] Open scholarship can involve making different stages of the workflow openly available, which can include the use of different formats to communicate early findings, observations, data sources, annotations, and final outputs. Each of these stages for the humanities may require different steps in the workflow lifecycle, from the collection of literature, artifacts, images, or recordings to data aggregation, annotation, analysis, critique, and summation. There are also implications for peer review, quality assurance, editing, communication, dissemination, and translation. It is often observed that, unlike the sciences, the humanities have a culture of individual rather than team-based research, with sole-authored rather than collaboratively produced outputs prioritized. While this aspect has been changing in some areas—such as the digital humanities, where collaborative research is often the norm—it remains the case in many fields.

One of the core characteristics and strengths of humanities research is the sheer diversity of disciplines encompassed, as well as different time periods, geographies, philosophies, languages, and cultures. The breadth of research that is covered by the term *humanities* is so extensive that the development of an open humanities culture provides a potential gateway to a vast wealth of new connections and collaborations—spanning disciplines including ancient and modern languages, history, archaeology, anthropology, geography, literature, law, politics, and religion, to list only a few. In practice, the humanities are made up of many and varied disciplines that each have their own agenda, history, and directions, and manifest differently around the world across languages and national systems. Consequently, the tangible products of the humanities tend to be quite different from those of the sciences and, as such, can be presented through a multitude of communication channels and formats. Source materials may be analog or digital and may exist in widely distributed forms online, as in the case of social media. Many bring with them complexities in terms of presentation and preservation, and intellectual property and copyright issues. Digital reappropriation, revision, or alteration—for example, of music and artwork—can pose particular problems that are not the same as in the sciences.[18] The sharing of data or digital content in the humanities, especially involving images, film, and recordings from secondary sources, may be subject to further laws and restrictions. Legal and technical barriers can also limit academics' capacity to deposit unreviewed materials such as datasets, primary materials, archival collections, images, and multimedia assets in repositories. Culturally sensitive information cannot be made open, as often is the case with Indigenous knowledge. While the sciences are also vast in scope and have a plethora of subspecializations, there has been stronger support at the discipline level for global coordination of science data sharing that again relates back to fundamental differences in how science research is undertaken, which has had the effect of further advantaging OS scholarship.

Open Access Publishing in the Humanities

The open scholarship movement began with a focus on OA publishing. Although much variation is present between disciplines, it is widely known that publishing and citation practices in the humanities are significantly different from those in the sciences. In the case of each discipline area, conventions have become established and entrenched. For the sciences, collaborative multiauthor publishing emphasizing and encouraging citation has served to speed up the circulation of new research for others to build upon further. This is one reason that publishing in the sciences has more immediately benefited from OA publishing models. Although open publication outlets for the humanities are gaining in prominence, relatively few humanities scholars are embracing these alternative channels.[19] Humanities scholars, by and large, continue to conform to traditional disciplinary publishing practices[20] that have emerged out of long-standing traditions of sole authorship, as noted, and an approach to research that is less concerned with the immediate spread of findings, or citation, and more with producing original and often necessarily longer-length, enduring works of scholarship. Despite a changing landscape, humanities scholars continue to value books over journal articles as the most prestigious outputs.[21] Indeed, humanities academic committees continue to place the highest value on book-length publications for job promotion, tenure, and grant funding.[22]

Various other reasons account for the lower uptake of OA publishing in the humanities, which relate to fundamental disciplinary differences, as well as a different trajectory of development over the past two decades since the beginning of the OA movement. Citation databases mostly cover journal articles rather than books and do not generally index book chapters. As such, some of the outputs most highly valued by researchers and institutions are not registered. Because publications in the sciences receive much wider coverage via citation, they can more easily be appraised through bibliometric counts.[23] In the long tradition of scientific publishing, citations have been regarded as a reliable measure of quality, but in the humanities they are less embedded and not as clearly aligned with traditions of research and publication. The humanities are then at a fundamental disadvantage if citation measures are used as a primary gauge of quality and impact.[24] The flow-on effect is that journal impact factors and overall citation rates in the humanities tend to be much lower than in the sciences,[25] and, considered alone, they are not a reliable indicator of the value or relevance of a published work. For researchers in the humanities, the result is that citation alone is not a strong motivator. The variety of topics, contemporary and historical, within the humanities means that there is a very wide potential readership across multiple areas, which is not adequately represented by the current citation system.[26] The intended audience for specialized scientific publications is generally narrower or more clearly defined than in the humanities, and again this means that the sciences are better suited to academic citation analysis. A further difference is that while research results in the sciences, notably the "exact sciences,"[27] are often treated as building blocks—with one set of findings directly enabling the next investigation—in the humanities, results are often less tangible and less solid. Researchers may not want to "build" at all but rather to disrupt established knowledge in the spirit of what Foucault referred to as an *"insurrection of subjugated knowledges,"*[28] or they may simply want to explore neglected, forgotten, or marginal areas of knowledge.

A publication on the topic of a newly discovered ancient human practice may initially have very few readers and even fewer citations in the short term, when compared with a work in the sciences responding to a pressing issue in the contemporary world. A rapidly produced, work-in-progress article on the topic of the next potential vaccine to protect against Covid-19 may be instantly read and referred to by millions around the world because of its relevance to that global issue—around which recent experience has demonstrated an unprecedented effort at coordination and data sharing. Yet conversely, humanities research publications can have a very long influence and a longer tail of value, which may even increase over time. A work produced today that is not widely cited and has little immediate impact may become highly influential in the future. Many institutional and national research assessment exercises ask a researcher to list their main published work over a five-year period, when in the humanities some researchers' most important and influential work could have been produced decades prior and, crucially, still be growing in relevance. These complex and interrelated factors concerning the differing cultures of publication and citation in the humanities and sciences point to wider questions linked with tensions between forms of assessment (discussed in Chapter 5).

The challenges are compounded by the fact that leading databases—such as Google Scholar, Scopus, and Web of Science—currently primarily index English-language publications and research outputs, yet many valuable works in the humanities appear in other languages. Many such works are not discoverable or available for wider access.[29] Equitable openness in this context must mean making works and publications available in multiple languages in translation, or providing robust tools for multilingualism, as noted in the UNESCO

Recommendation on Open Science of 2021. Through embracing multilingual practices and formats, digital platforms and tools can help to preserve and sustain local languages and their cultural history, which also has implications for the communication channels that might be used to reach the participants or potential recipients of the research, in regional communities. While the dominance of English as the language of scholarly publication is also an issue in the sciences,[30] the problems of second-language delivery and access are heightened in the humanities across many disciplines because of their stronger focus on social and cultural matters rather than empirical findings. Led by the humanities, bibliodiversity is becoming a fundamental dimension of open scholarship, producing locally relevant knowledge, informing public debate, and helping build more inclusive societies.[31]

Other related factors set the humanities apart from the sciences in terms of OA publishing. Due to being at different stages in the development of open practices, there is greater representation of the sciences in open publishing. There is not yet an equivalent, for example, of the highly ranked not-for-profit OA mega-journal *PLOS ONE* published by the Public Library of Science. Many in the humanities consider newer OA publishers to be of lower quality than the established, top-tier commercial print publishers,[32] perpetuating a conservative publication culture.[33] "Predatory" publishers—many of them initially difficult to identify—have complicated this situation by confusing legitimate OA initiatives with a dubious publishing landscape that requires authors to pay OA fees while not guaranteeing adequate peer review, leading to potential reputational disadvantages or worse; publication in such outlets may actively work against a humanities researcher's career. Many humanities scholars continue to be resistant to OA publishing, in part due to lack of information or clear direction, but also owing to concerns about intellectual property, copyright licensing, plagiarism, and legitimacy of OA platforms.[34] There is a limit to how effective or comprehensive OA mandates for funded research will be in the humanities and social sciences, where unfunded research is extensive.[35]

There are typically fewer sources of funding for OA in the humanities.[36] As noted, the basic issue of affordability puts OA options beyond the reach of many working in the humanities, where budgets typically cannot cover article processing charges (APCs) or book processing charges (BPCs), and where institutions provide limited support outside the sciences. Overall, the funding issue has widened the gap between institutions that can and those that cannot afford this additional level of support. Open access subsidies are typically focused on the sciences, and on highly ranked journals, of which there are far fewer in the humanities. Some niche areas have no such journals, and even relatively mainstream humanities disciplines may have only a handful, possibly with multiyear wait times to publication. Taking into account the across-the-board lack of funding for OA journal publishing in the humanities, the even greater expense of openly publishing books is an insurmountable barrier for most, even in institutions in developed countries.[37] Here again, the tradition of publishing long-form works in the humanities disadvantages the field when compared with the sciences, in the current context of a world moving toward open scholarship. Many observers would then point out that the cost of publishing in prestigious scientific journals can be extortionate, yet the cost for the research itself is also much higher in the sciences. The humanities sector was caught off guard by the mandates introduced to ensure that government-funded research be made open. The reality is that areas of the sciences had been preparing for this and already shifting their funding model to enable the transition.[38] While the sciences quickly began to adapt by building the costs of APCs into research budgets, the humanities have had a less-coordinated approach and less capacity to do so.

However, despite all these differences in disciplinary cultures and the many challenges that have slowed uptake of open scholarship, major progress has been made toward establishing OA publishing services in the humanities. Open access publishing platforms—such as the Open Library of Humanities (OLH), Open Book Publishers, Open Humanities Press, OpenEdition, Knowledge Unlatched, Ubiquity Press, and Language Science Press—are developing new approaches to assist in covering the APCs and BPCs of OA. The Conversation, a not-for-profit network linking academics and journalists, enables humanities researchers to publish short topical articles under Creative Commons licensing, making findings and commentary rapidly available to much wider audiences. In addition to open publishing services, numerous bibliographic databases and digital platforms are emerging. In the humanities, these include the long-established Social Sciences Research Network (owned by Elsevier publishers since 2016), the Center for Open Science, and the highly recognized SciELO (Scientific Electronic Library Online network). The OAPEN (Open Access Publishing in European Networks) online library and publications platform is supporting the Directory of Open Access Books (DOAB). Open programs for free access to publications after the initial embargo, together with open repository aggregators of digital materials like OpenAIRE in Europe and LA Referencia in South America, support the discovery of open research outputs by collecting, organizing, and systematizing information on OA publications. Open Methods is providing access to the raw descriptions of methods, results, data, and code to make the entire research process more transparent. In other examples, the Open Content Alliance, Internet Archive, and institutions such as the British Library, Digital Public Library of America, and National Library of Australia (to mention only a few) now have ongoing projects to create permanent, publicly accessible archives of digitized texts.[39]

The contrast presented here between the humanities and the sciences is not to reinforce a difference or disagreement but rather to ask the question: how can humanities best benefit from and situate its publication practices within this changing environment for the greatest impact and reach of research outputs? Without adequate incentives, training, and funding for open scholarship (as discussed in the previous chapter), humanities researchers face the risk of missing the opportunity to play a leading role in setting future directions not only in their field but potentially across the many disciplines, cultures, and communities where their work could be made visible and accessible.

Collecting, Sustaining, and Sharing Humanities Data

While making data openly available has become increasingly common in the sciences, special challenges apply for the humanities.[40] Humanities researchers draw upon large amounts of data, but few interpret or define this as "data" and are therefore less likely to systematically record it in a structured digital format that is readily understandable and usable by others.[41] Many consider data as necessarily quantitative or numerical and would say that the term *data* oversimplifies the complex phenomena and often highly specialized material dealt with in the humanities.[42] Yet data can be understood as consisting of not just lists, tables, or matrices with organized, numerical, categorical, or ordinal information, but also all materials collected, produced, compiled, and used throughout stages of the research workflow life cycle.[43] Data can comprise, for example, archival documents, cultural artifacts, oral histories, photographs, art, and audio and video recordings. Drawing on digital humanities methods, structured data can be analyzed using techniques such as data mining, modeling and visualization, deep mapping, network analysis, text encoding, and many other applications.[44]

Breakthroughs in computing have opened the way for quicker analysis and greater accuracy using very large datasets. The scientific response to address Covid-19 has shown the value of rapid data sharing. Engagement with big data has been essential for medical research and for many other areas of the sciences, yet across the humanities it is far less common. Humanities research often involves small-scale, diverse datasets produced by a sole researcher,[45] working, for example, in local contexts or language-specific communities. Although the humanities may not have the scale of data to match the sciences and may not seek it, massive quantities of cultural material and collections have been digitized over the last three decades, led by major institutions. However, these sources can sometimes be difficult to make openly available due to copyright or related restrictions, which may apply to material held in galleries, libraries, archives, and museums (GLAM), for example. This is further complicated in the case of "orphan works" where there may be limited knowledge of ownership[46] or legal guidelines for sharing.[47]

An issue that is particularly relevant in the humanities is that protection of sensitive personal data cannot always be guaranteed through anonymity.[48] In such cases, "mediated access" as opposed to full OA can be used to ensure data integrity, often through password protection, allowing only some data to be used and reused by authorized parties and through the signing of ethical agreements. Publishers are increasingly calling for data availability statements (DAS) to show where datasets can be located and whether any restrictions apply. The All European Academies (ALLEA) has published a number of reports on how to harness open scholarship in the humanities.[49] The report on "Sustainable and FAIR Data Sharing in the Humanities"[50] offers recommendations for humanities data management. In some cases, there may be a need to consider possible limits to openness—for example, in safeguarding Indigenous knowledge by respecting cultural protocols and data sovereignty. The collective benefit, authority to control, responsibility, ethics (CARE) principles for Indigenous data governance were formulated in 2018 to specifically address Indigenous data sovereignty and stewardship. This recognizes the fundamental right of Indigenous peoples to control their cultural knowledge in digital environments in view of inherent "power differentials and historical contexts." The CARE principles affirm "the right to create value from Indigenous data in ways that are grounded in Indigenous worldviews."[51]

Compiling and maintaining humanities data requires substantial funding, but the case is harder to make to governments and other funders because the return on investment is less clear or direct than in the sciences. Gathering data in medical research often has a well-defined goal with a direct, measurable benefit for human health. It is more difficult to quantify the value of fostering and maintaining cultural memory.[52] Yet collection of cultural data in digital form not only preserves culture but also assigns, confirms, and helps build cultural value and resilience. Investment in humanities data is not an investment in knowledge of the physical world but of the world of thought, memory, emotion, imagination, creativity, belief, and ritual—in other words, the realm of human culture.[53]

Humanities Infrastructure

Long-term digital infrastructure is essential for all aspects of open scholarship, including for publication, data sharing, integration, documentation, and analysis, as well as for digital preservation. Infrastructures work at different scales, varying in purpose and function. They may bring together materials and centralize data, or link outward to external sources.[54] They generally provide a discovery mechanism, so that digital assets and collections can be registered and found. Whatever their specific characteristics or goals, digital platforms of all kinds rely on comprehensive descriptive metadata for information to be accessible and reusable.

In humanities research, infrastructures take many forms, yet as noted in the broader open scholarship context, this sector has not had the opportunity to develop such platforms as rapidly as the sciences. Infrastructure is often thought of in terms of equipment or facilities, but for the humanities, until only a few decades ago, the physical holdings of libraries and museums were the primary support system for research. Now, in the digital realm, there are multiple forms of infrastructure, enabling new kinds of research and providing interactive spaces and environments. The 2020 Principles of Open Scholarly Infrastructure (POSI)[55] set out to expand the range of infrastructural discussions beyond an emphasis on the sciences, noting, "In some parts of the world, science and technology are increasingly seen as being out-of-touch with the ethical, social, and cultural concerns of the communities within which they operate. We are concerned that infrastructures that focus exclusively on 'science' will simply further entrench the 'two cultures' divide and exacerbate this trend."[56]

The open publishing platforms that have been referred to in this book are forms of infrastructure, as are institutional repositories. Openly available digitized source materials are increasingly being used as foundational resources for humanities research. Typically, humanities infrastructures draw together large collections of content and data and provide a connective environment for open discovery, access, investigation, and user contribution. They may be discipline-specific or thematically focused on a multifaceted issue. The value of digital infrastructures lies not only in the capacity to hold and accumulate knowledge but also in the capacity to bring together otherwise fragmented collections and initiatives, pooling resources and enabling new sorts of inquiry.[57]

The means to facilitate open solutions in the humanities have grown significantly over the past decade, with the backing of major consortia including GLAM institutions that are also supporting publicly accessible archives of digitized texts and offering integrated tools for their analysis. Some of the most recognized infrastructures are the multi-country partnerships and platforms across Europe. They include Common Language Resources and Technology Infrastructure (CLARIN),[58] Digital Research Infrastructure for the Arts and Humanities (DARIAH),[59] Europeana,[60] European Research Infrastructure for Heritage Science (E-RIHS),[61] Open Access Infrastructure for Research in Europe (OpenAIRE),[62] and Open Scholarly Communication for the Social Sciences and the Humanities in the European Research Area for Social Sciences and Humanities (OPERAS).[63] These are only a sample of extensive global activity.

A fundamental feature of much infrastructure for the humanities is enabling communities of interest and practice.[64] Humanities Commons, launched in 2016 with the support of the Modern Language Association and a grant from the Andrew W. Mellon Foundation in the United States, is an example of a people-centered collaborative network.[65] Collecting institutions are playing a central role in reaching wider audiences and accelerating OA to online resources through approaches that are greatly improving the availability and reusability of their digitized collections and source materials.[66] Many such organizations are championing open sharing of cultural memory and history, often through collaborative projects developed in conjunction with university researchers. Time Machine,[67] for example, is an ambitious large-scale digitization and computing consortium established to use big data to help map, preserve, and gain new understanding of European history over time; it has also extended to other geographical contexts.[68]

Use of digital infrastructure can help promote diverse perspectives, including supporting multilingual research. The Canadian Humanities and Social Sciences Commons (Canadian HSS Commons)[69] is a national bilingual network for distributing open materials and projects, supporting social scholarship. Looking at further initiatives from other parts of the world, the South African Centre for Digital Language Resources (SADiLaR)[70] is systematically digitizing and making available research data and educational programs related to the eleven official languages of South Africa. In India, where there are twenty-two official languages, Knowledge Sharing in Publishing (KSHIP)[71] has been established as an open multilingual scholarly publishing platform for the humanities and social sciences.[72] The Pacific and Regional Archive for Digital Sources in Endangered Cultures (PARADISEC)[73] focuses on preserving endangered languages and associated cultural expressions. Time-Layered Cultural Map (TLCMap)[74] is another Australian example—a spatiotemporal infrastructure serving a wide variety of projects. The recently launched Australian Research Data Commons (ARDC) project HASS and Indigenous Research Data Commons aims to produce digital platforms and analysis tools to improve access to Australia's HASS (humanities, arts, and social sciences) and Indigenous knowledge, with an emphasis on Indigenous data sovereignty.[75] Australia, where this book's authors are based, has other established infrastructures, such as Austlit,[76] AusStage,[77] Design and Art Australia Online,[78] and the Humanities Networked Infrastructure (HuNI).[79]

Societal and cultural divides of all kinds are manifest in computing practices and in data selection, development, cost structures, and many other facets of humanities infrastructure. Aggregating data from numerous sources can reveal patterns that were previously invisible, making inherent biases, omissions, and power relations more apparent.[80] This is especially the case when historical documentation is digitized and made openly available. Centuries of collecting regimes, with their priorities and blind spots, gaps, erasures, and silences, come into clearer focus. With increasing engagement by humanities communities in the processes of incorporating broader input into the design of infrastructure, steps are being taken toward recognizing and reimagining open scholarly systems as bearers of cultural values and agents of social change.[81]

Community-Based Open Knowledge

For centuries, academics, researchers, curators, and collectors have collaborated with engaged members of the community—"gifted amateurs"—in what is now called *citizen science*. Among the most well-known cases was the British government's offer in 1714 of a monetary prize to anyone who could come up with a way of measuring a ship's longitudinal position.[82] In 1879, the *Oxford English Dictionary* appealed to the public to supply lexicographers with the spelling, definitions, and meanings of rare words in magazines, journals, books, letters, and newspapers.[83] There are many other examples around the world. In the mid-1990s, citizen science was conceived of as research that is partially or wholly conducted by nonspecialist volunteers. It can be defined as "projects in which volunteers and scientists work together to answer real-world questions."[84] Interaction between experts and the public grew dramatically when the internet enabled real-time exchange of ideas and content. It is instructive to recall Tim Berners-Lee's comment: "The Web is more a social creation than a technical one. I designed it for a social effect—to help people work together—and not as a technical toy."[85] Communities can play an active role in problem-solving, communication, and knowledge translation through open cooperation.[86] Community-based open knowledge, in all its forms, has particular relevance for the humanities, especially in terms of the current "impact" agenda that is encouraging researchers to respond to pressing contemporary concerns and show how their investigations are making a difference and engaging the public. Academics are experimenting with *citizen humanities* approaches that support and value connecting with communities "to engage with members of the public who may not be traditionally aligned with, or an expected audience for, academic work."[87]

Related to citizen science, the term *crowdsourcing* was coined by Jeff Howe, editor of *Wired*, in 2006.[88] He described how businesses could use the internet not only for "outsourcing" their work but also for "crowdsourcing" it. This can be defined as "the use of available platforms and communications networks to distribute tasks amongst large numbers of interested individuals, working towards a common goal."[89] Enlisting virtual crowds has enabled organizations to reduce costs and enhance economies of scale through co-creation.[90] Established online crowdsourcing services such as Amazon Mechanical Turk,[91] Microworkers,[92] and Zooniverse[93] host myriad projects, with volunteers (paid and unpaid) completing tasks that technology alone cannot achieve.[94] Like citizen science, crowdsourcing projects can delegate jobs to the public such as collecting, cataloging, and annotating, or invite input through involvement in the entire process from conceptualizing, framing, and setting up a research agenda and methodology to analyzing outcomes.[95] These processes and relationships are also referred to using other terms such as *collective intelligence, communal and peer engagement, crowd wisdom, mass collaboration, participatory practice,* and *user-powered systems.*

The wealth of local and firsthand knowledge that can be crowdsourced adds depth and detail to social and cultural projects where individual and situated experience can provide crucial understanding. For the humanities, this can include participation in a range of tasks, such as transcribing handwritten text;

correcting digitized content; categorizing and cataloging information with structured, descriptive metadata; collaborative tagging; implicit and explicit linking of data; providing contextual details for artifacts; locating complementary objects to be included in an online collection; recording memories and intangible heritage; commenting and offering critical reflections; mapping visual, spatial, and cultural representations; translating content; and co-curation.[96] The "crowd" within humanities and cultural heritage crowdsourcing projects does not necessarily comprise large groups of people but can be a small number of interested and engaged citizens who may already have a relationship with the topic in question.[97] "Nichesourcing" targets a niche community with identifiable proficiency or background.[98]

Crowdsourcing can provide input where information or expertise is limited. The world's largest reference work, Wikipedia,[99] is an example of mass online public contribution that has shifted the boundaries between knowledge creation and dissemination.[100] The Transcribe Bentham project, started in 2010, is an early exemplar of crowdsourcing in the humanities.[101] CrowdHeritage[102]—an open platform assisted by the European Commission—is using crowdsourcing to improve the metadata of Europeana.[103] Some of the most successful initiatives have been developed in the GLAM sector to encourage members of the public as volunteers and communities of interest to interact with, explore, and interpret, contextualize, and enrich collections. Trove, at the National Library of Australia, is regarded as a world-leading example of crowdsourcing.[104] Planned in 2008 as a portal to the National Library of Australia's discovery services, it has become highly successful, with volunteers correcting the optical character recognition (OCR)-digitized content of Australian newspapers. To date, the public program has seen over 430 million lines of text corrected.[105]

Along with the benefits, crowdsourcing presents known challenges. Ethical issues around "free labor" remain a concern.[106] There are also hidden costs,[107] as involving participants can be complex and time-consuming, requiring purpose-designed platforms and interfaces, and systems for checking, moderating, and processing contributed materials. Even so, crowdsourcing represents one of the most visible and widespread examples of two-way open humanities in action. The capacity to empower community members through seeking and utilizing their input to add to or modify existing understandings sets it apart from the kind of open approach that permits entry into spaces where scholarly knowledge can be viewed but not altered. By allowing movement in both directions with the public, crowdsourcing offers one of the more free and democratic types of openness.

Many forms of open scholarship, despite growing uptake, are not generally recognized by the systems that evaluate research performance and impact in universities. The next chapter addresses the issue of institutional reporting and measurement, which relies heavily on traditional bibliometric and citation data, and makes the case for changes in policies and practice to acknowledge the relevance and value of open approaches in the contemporary world.

5

Reshaping How Universities Assess Research Impact

This chapter explores tensions between university policies that aim to increase and demonstrate research impact through external engagement, and the continued emphasis on appraising academic excellence at the individual, discipline, and national levels according to conventional bibliometric methods and citation analysis. The discussion considers a range of issues influencing research assessment processes and indicates how changes in evaluation, including greater use of altmetrics and open peer review, might foster further uptake of open scholarship.

Bibliometrics and Impact Factors

A paper published in the journal *Science* in 1927 is regarded as the first to use citation counts as an indicator of the significance of scientific research.[1] The practice of citing the work of others grew along with the increasing number of scholarly publications, especially the exponential rise in the number of academic articles appearing after the Second World War.[2] In 1964, American linguist Eugene Garfield pioneered the Science Citation Index, designed for systematic tracking of citations between papers.[3] For libraries needing to carefully consider which publications to prioritize for purchase, such an index made it possible to know not only the number of citations of an individual article but also those relating to a particular journal, thereby facilitating both author and journal "impact factors," as they would become known.

The term *bibliometrics*, first used in 1934 to describe "the measurement of all aspects related to the publication and reading of books and documents,"[4] now refers to a vast field of statistical inquiry. Underpinned by the rapid data sharing made possible by online publishing and the internet, citation analysis is an ever-growing field. Whereas citations were previously extracted manually, nowadays automated analysis tools are used to compute various impact measures, drawing on millions of citations to illustrate and map large-scale patterns across different disciplines, including the reach and influence of the most highly cited scholarly articles. Automated systems are sophisticated and relatively inexpensive, and provide easily accessible, instant, objective, and replicable results that can be scaled up from single researcher to faculty, university, and whole-of-country outputs. The h-index was developed in 2005 to rank authors based on their publication activity and citation levels.[5]

The widespread use of new systems for automated citation indexing has led to even greater dependence on the use of citation analysis for assessing research significance and influence. Despite the prevalence and efficacy of such analysis, however, there is criticism of the reliance on bibliometrics as an accurate and independent indicator of research quality. Mounting commentary suggests that these measures are theoretically weak, time dependent, highly platform-specific, unsuitable for many subject areas, and limiting in terms of language and accessibility; moreover, they risk oversimplification or misrepresentation.[6] Citation counts, impact factors, and the h-index may be poorly interpreted or misused,[7] and sole reliance on publication-related citation data can at best offer a one-dimensional understanding of the value of research. A long-running and principal concern relates to why a publication is being cited.[8] There are very different possible motivations for citing the work of others. A citation may be supportive, used to provide an example, outline a theory or methodology, or illustrate a new creative work; however, it might also be negative and critical of the source cited.[9] Mainstream topics tend to generate more citations,[10] and there is a possibility of lowered standards driven by competition to be visible regardless of quality.[11]

Evaluating Scholarly Work

Over the past two decades, there have been growing calls worldwide by government and funding agencies for universities to demonstrate the value and significance of their research—for greater accountability and transparency, and to justify public investment. Mandates to provide open access (OA) to outputs are a key response.[12] Although many funding bodies acknowledge and value translational research and cross-sector partnerships, universities continue to adhere to a career progression framework that rewards researchers based on individual achievements and values conventional publications (in many disciplines giving priority to sole or first authorships) over digital products or tools designed for wider knowledge dissemination and reuse.[13]

The long-standing publish-or-perish culture remains one of the most significant disincentives to open practices, with deep-seated biases toward prestigious publishers that committees judge favorably for tenure and promotion.[14] Open practices, especially those that fall outside traditional reward systems, run the risk of negatively influencing faculty evaluation and harming career advancement.[15] Many perceive the self-archiving of research in institutional repositories as a cumbersome administrative requirement rather than a way of maximizing the value and reach of their work.[16] Even those who are aware of OA options may only selectively experiment with them, following for the most part traditional publication practices. This has led to a situation where "one of the most noticeable current themes in the OA field is that there continue to be significant levels of disinterest, suspicion, and scepticism about OA amongst researchers."[17] For the performance of academics and universities to be considered in terms of the contribution they make in society, universities will need to reshape their assessment processes to acknowledge those who engage in outreach activities and open scholarship. To implement this shift in focus, innovative approaches and evaluative frameworks are required for capturing different forms of impact to show how research has improved society, culture, the economy, the environment, health, and quality of life—in other words, how these public benefits have occurred because of this new knowledge.

Formal research evaluation schemes at the national level are starting to place more weight on evidence and illustration of the contribution that academics play in addressing key issues in society. The UK Research Excellence Framework (REF) is a notable example.[18] It has explicitly set out that panels are not required to use conventional measures of publication channels, publisher classifications, journal impact factors, rankings, or lists to judge the quality of outputs.[19] Similarly, the European Commission, a major proponent of open scholarship, has trialed various models, including using inventories of case studies to assess societal influence of scholarly outputs, applying process evaluation and criteria developed for fields of inquiry as well as career stage.[20] In the United States, the Crowdsourcing and Citizen Science Act of 2015[21] indicates that citizens should be encouraged to actively participate in research projects and in setting agendas and also be involved in evaluation.[22] Such models have raised awareness of the need to adapt research measurement according to different disciplinary fields and jurisdictions, as well as broader socioeconomic objectives.[23]

Assessment regimes in general, however, have remained slow to adapt. Entrenched systems of measurement, evaluation, and ranking directly determine the flows of federal funding in most national systems, and so a fresh outlook is required for there to be a change in policy and practice. While bibliometric indicators are likely to remain the dominant form of scholarly evaluation used by universities to appraise research quality, new ways of valuing engagement beyond citation metrics or publisher prestige are also needed. Traditional bibliometrics have limited capacity to show where original ideas and findings have been put into practice and how effective solutions have been, and they are not equally suited to all disciplines.[24] Assessing scholarly communication should also recognize and acknowledge different types of scholarly work. There are calls for more responsible use of metrics in general, as illustrated in recent policy documents, such as the San Francisco Declaration on Research Assessment (DORA),[25] the Leiden Manifesto for Research Metrics,[26] and the Metric Tide Report.[27]

Altmetrics for Assessment

Alternative metrics—or altmetrics—have emerged over the past decade, aligned with the open scholarship movement, as a means of evaluating research activities from open sources.[28] The term was introduced in "Altmetrics: A Manifesto"[29] in 2010 and defined by its authors as "the creation and study of new metrics based on the social web for analyzing and informing scholarship."[30] Altmetrics draw from a greater variety of data and sources, and also enable evaluation of a richer selection of end products, not only publications.[31] Altmetrics can be described as a subset of scholarly metrics that include "indicators based on recorded events of acts (e.g., viewing, reading, saving, diffusing, mentioning, citing, reusing, modifying) related to scholarly documents (e.g., papers, books, blog posts, datasets, code) or scholarly agents (e.g., researchers, universities, funders, journals)."[32]

The social web, with its many applications, fosters participation, interaction, and user-generated content.[33] For researchers, it can become a central aspect of scholarly communication, enabling them to actively connect with one another, build their profile, and freely disseminate ideas and findings to a larger audience. This can lead to increased communication and collaboration with the public, and as discussed in the previous chapter, it can encourage greater citizen participation in the design, planning, and implementation of research. Yet while most academics are aware of social networking services and tools, only some routinely use these to develop or promote their work.[34] This is due in part to a perceived lack of trustworthiness related to underlying concerns about the commercial nature of many such services,[35] and it can also be a result of time constraints, uncertainty about which platforms are most effective, and lack of recognition in the university system.[36]

Online networking services such as Academia, ResearchGate, and LinkedIn, among plenty of others, each with different features, are providing online spaces and communities that support open scholarship in various ways. Unlike automated aggregators of bibliometric data, these services give more agency and control to researchers in how they present their work and to which audiences. The use of mainstream social media also encourages openness and sharing and helps build connections and networks, often reaching an even broader public. While circulation of published material is subject to the regulations and requirements of publishers, these platforms are offering alternatives to traditional publication channels and use of citation indices for assessing performance. Studies have shown that professionals, government, industry, and the public all access and use research but rarely cite academic publications.[37] The social web offers opportunities to capture how wider society is sharing and discussing scholarly works.[38]

The emphasis in altmetrics is on developing indicators that can reliably and validly determine the impact of scholarly works by observing and measuring various community user activities in online environments.[39] Altmetric measures include the extent and frequency of collaboration and interaction between researchers, multidisciplinary stakeholders, and the broader community, such as through community, radio, television, and media presentations; outreach events; and public influence stories via university websites and social media.[40] These alternative metrics can also help universities in their efforts to overcome any negative "ivory tower" image by tracking website views, usage, circulation of content, and multiple other forms of public participation, including engagement with open online courses. Case studies can be used to map the contexts and time frames in which researchers and community stakeholders engage.[41]

There has been a notable expansion in the breadth and depth of available data for altmetrics, which can be sourced from numerous services such as Altmetric .com, Crossref Event Data, ImpactStory (formerly Total-Impact), PLOS Article-Level Metrics, and Plum Analytics.[42] These collate data and display indicators of how users are accessing scholarly works, and the extent to which academics are engaging in conversations with a broader public audience.[43] For example, Plum

Analytics aggregates five categories—citations, usage, captures, mentions, and social media—for sixty-seven different types of scholarly outputs that include journal articles, books, and datasets, as well as code/software, conference papers, designs, grants, live performances, presentations, press releases, standards, syllabi, visual arts, and videos, along with many others.[44] Working closely with publishers, Altmetric.com is another popular service that sources, tracks, and reports metrics for a wide range of outputs.[45]

Yet despite the apparent benefits, altmetrics have their own challenges. Whereas bibliometric data are relatively static, and biases and errors can be corrected, altmetric data sources are dynamic, and usage changes continually, so data for the tracking of engagement can quickly become outdated. As such, accuracy, consistency, and replicability are major issues.[46] Linking social media use with societal influence can also be subjective and problematic.[47] Given that "there is no international methodological standard for assessing societal impact," it is likely that "simplistic metrics will prevail and will discourage research on strongly desirable societal objectives."[48] While social media platforms have broad socioeconomic, demographic, and geographic reach, users are not representative of the general public. Moreover, like conventional bibliometrics, altmetric providers also focus on numerical scores to gauge usage or attention and rely on digital object identifiers (DOIs) or other identifiers that are typically assigned to traditional outputs.[49] Other challenges include differences in how data are sourced and analyzed, and the fact that most altmetrics services are owned by for-profit companies.[50]

Even despite these issues, the use of altmetrics can be regarded as a more open and transparent option than standard bibliometrics, allowing new insights and also encouraging productive interaction and communication between academic and community stakeholders. Measuring attention does not necessarily indicate uptake or impact but, arguably, better illustrates the activity of scholarly communication. Hence, a combination of traditional bibliometric data based on citations complemented by altmetrics can give a fuller picture of societal influence.[51]

Open Peer Review

From the time peer review was first introduced, single- and double-blind review of publications has evolved into a rigorous and agreed-upon system for the effective scrutiny and validation of original research, ensuring expert-endorsed publication of findings.[52] Recently, however, the value of long-established peer review approaches has been questioned. Concerns relate to the choice of reviewers, their credibility, the time it takes to complete the review process, and the emphasis sometimes placed on a publication's "technical soundness rather than on its novelty, originality, or significance."[53] Proponents of open scholarship have made the case that the peer review process should be more transparent, for knowledge claims to be as robust as possible, and more interactive, to allow a dynamic culture of debate during and after publication, avoiding "gatekeeping."[54]

In this context, open peer review is evolving as a viable alternative to typical peer review. As a general principle, this form of peer review identifies the names of reviewers, making reviewer selection, and often their comments, transparent and attributable. However, there are currently no accepted understandings of what constitutes open peer review, so some ambiguity remains. For example, while open peer review generally reveals the identity of authors and reviewers, it does not always do so.[55] Reviewer reports might be made openly available, but the names of reviewers may not be linked directly with individual reports. Even so, those in favor contend that open peer review adds accountability at all levels and gives clearer credit to the work of reviewing, acknowledging the time and commitment that reviewers provide to the process.[56]

In some settings, open peer review can enable representatives of the broader community to evaluate, discuss, and add comments reflecting on a work's merits or shortcomings, in addition to the comments of specialists.[57] For example, *F1000Research* provides consecutive versions of manuscripts along with reviewers' comments, as well as scholarly reflections from readers, "recreating a scholarly dialogue."[58] A further example is the hybrid print/digital book series Debates in the Digital Humanities, which allows registered readers to annotate and comment directly on sections of text, representing a form of critical commentary.[59] The process of open peer review can also be applied outside of more familiar contexts of journals or published books, in relation to online self-publishing, including academic networking websites and social media. Here again, altmetrics offer a legitimate option for evaluating the extent to which scholars are sharing their works. While self-publishing is not valued in regular scholarly terms, for some it may be a means to make their work more widely and immediately available without relinquishing rights or paying excessive fees to traditional publishers.[60]

As this chapter has shown, new options are emerging and evolving for assessing research impact in ways that can productively support the open scholarship movement, but much work remains. The culture shift that is necessary has begun, but old systems and conventions are deeply embedded and tenacious, not only in institutions but also in the attitudes of individual researchers for whom recognition and advancement have traditionally depended on individual success and, in the case of humanities, where the highest measure of successful scholarship has been the publication of a sole-authored book by a highly rated publisher. This has fostered a culture of solitary endeavor with outputs valued for their quality but not necessarily their capacity to reach others and potentially enrich people's knowledge, understanding, and attitudes.

Conclusion: Pathways to Action

The open scholarship movement has undergone a profound transformation since its beginnings in the early twenty-first century, from a theoretical concept and call to action to an essential principle for research dissemination. The vision embodied by the BBB declarations—of knowledge being made more freely accessible and usable for research purposes and to the broader public—has come to be a reality and is expanding. The open scholarship drive has coincided with a period of massive growth and globalization of the research sector and of higher education.[1] During this time, as academic approaches and outputs have become increasingly digitalized, numerous aspects of scholarly communication have also evolved, with wide-ranging impacts on conventional formats and modalities used to present and utilize research. Three decades after the launch of the internet, advances in information, computing, and data technologies have reconfigured human interaction and social behaviors, including how we create and transmit knowledge.[2] Possibilities are multiplying with new breakthroughs in artificial intelligence (AI), surveillance, robotics, the Internet of Things, 3D printing, nanotechnology, biotechnology, and quantum theory, among a plethora of other areas.[3] All will likely have a bearing on the future of openness in society.

The field of open scholarship is again at a transitional moment due to the pace of change. The recent surge of activity outlined in earlier chapters particularly affects those disciplines that have been slower adopters, further widening the noted gap between the humanities and sciences. As institutions currently seek to fulfill the requirements of Plan S and other related mandates, major shifts are taking place nationally and internationally, aimed at reworking regulation, policy, funding models, and information and communications technology (ICT) development to achieve organizational and behavioral change. The core impulse of open scholarship, however, remains: to reshape the information environment so that academic inquiry can have the greatest impact for society.

Fundamentally, open scholarship wants to secure maximum collective value for investment in generating knowledge and learning by better connecting global research communities; by growing visibility, shareability, and discoverability of results; and by strengthening methods and practices in order to make findings more available and efficiently distributed, and able to be reused and adapted by wider publics with as few restrictions as possible.

Most academics are aware of open access (OA), and many individuals and institutions are drawing on tools, resources, and frameworks for implementation and governance of open scholarship, including engaging with publishers in introducing alternative business models. In universities, established research approaches, disciplinary standards, and cultures of work continue to be rethought across all domains. Aided by fast technological innovation and the capacity to produce and analyze data that were previously unavailable or not findable, new mechanisms for evaluation and impact assessment are being developed to gauge the reach and influence of research, including giving greater recognition for open practices and external engagement. Embracing open scholarship can come at a cost to researchers and their institutions, especially in the humanities, due to systemic barriers. To move toward a culture that rewards openly sharing information will require modifying the existing review, promotion, and tenure criteria to explicitly recognize public engagement and knowledge transfer. In the process of encouraging the uptake of policy at individual, faculty, library, and university levels, there is a necessity for increased commitment to staff education and the ICT platforms required for effective open scholarship, as well as the provision of financial and career incentives. Universities can stimulate positive change by clearly promoting policies around issues such as OA publishing and open peer review, and equipping academics with the skills and means to be able to benefit from the use of leading-edge infrastructure to significantly engage with and support this global paradigm shift.

Although the challenges are numerous, open scholarship is riding a wave of global acceptance and expansion. The digital environment offers new opportunities for outreach and collaboration that have barely begun to be properly explored. From the outset, the vision for openness has underscored the need for pathways for just, rightful, and inclusive information access for all citizens. Many factors have reduced access to knowledge, relating to socioeconomic circumstances, location, ethnicity, language, gender, age, and others. Open scholarship aims to address these and other barriers wherever possible. Critics have noted that although more research literature may now be freely retrievable through institutional repositories, this does not make it comprehensible to all the potential users, particularly the broader public.[4] While questions persist around whether open scholarship can be truly democratic, the potential benefits are indisputable. Barriers to openness vary widely in different settings, with many challenges prevalent across the humanities, but in order to navigate these and maximize the gains, they need to be identified and addressed by institutional policymakers.

While open scholarship is a worldwide movement with the chance to provide substantial benefits for universities, businesses, government, and nongovernmental organizations,[5] it also involves a complex array of power relations that may not always be consistent with the goal of inclusive, equitable development. On the macro level, open scholarship policies have stemmed primarily from the Global North, creating new categories of exclusion with the prospect of exacerbating colonialist legacies in systems of scholarly communication and further disadvantaging already marginalized groups.[6] The rhetoric of openness-as-equity-and-democracy risks hiding very real imbalances. Being open does not equate to being unprejudiced or nondiscriminatory. Openness is not equity, but it can be a step toward it. Openness can expose inherent biases and make them more transparent.

This book has identified key issues, highlighting them where possible from the perspective of the humanities. We believe that the humanities can play a particularly important role in encouraging open scholarship from a standpoint that is different from that of the sciences in that its disciplines fundamentally direct their attention more toward the human rather than the scientific values of the knowledge spectrum. The book does not lay claim to solving the issues raised and has not prescribed a particular means of doing so. It speaks to individual and institutional pressures and contexts, and to globally relevant dimensions of a wide range of concerns by acknowledging them and choosing examples from different parts of the world to actively emphasize linguistic, cultural, and economic factors.

We also argue that to be effectual in the long term, open scholarship must be considered and fostered at a whole-of-system level—involving individuals, groups, and institutions—rather than seeing issues in isolation. By recognizing and addressing the barriers collaboratively with stakeholders, universities can lead the way in changing their culture and policy through long-term strategies.[7] This requires more coordination and cooperation with national and international research councils, funding bodies, communities, and industry to produce and implement action plans, and to compel change not only at the institutional level but also, just as importantly, in the broader civic context.[8] The opening up of research is a two-way process, providing for citizen input as well as making expert research publicly available. The future success of the open scholarship movement will be dependent on extending and maintaining these pathways to facilitate access to the global arena of knowledge creation and to the treasure troves of the world's research.

Notes

Introduction: Unlocking Scholarship

1   Council of Australian University Librarians, "CAUL Statement on Open Scholarship 2019," 2019, 2, https://www.caul.edu.au/programs-projects/advancing-open-scholarship-fair/statement-open-scholarship. In this book, we choose to use the term *open scholarship* to emphasize principles of openness. A range of related terms are often used interchangeably, including *digital scholarship*, which Lewis et al. define as "the creation, production, analysis, or publishing and dissemination of new scholarship using digital or computational techniques." Vivian Lewis, Lisa Spiro, Xuemao Wang, and Jon E. Cawthorne, *Building Expertise to Support Digital Scholarship: A Global Perspective* (Washington, DC: Council on Library and Information Resources, 2015), 1, https://www.clir.org/pubs/reports/pub168/.
2   Alyssa Arbuckle, Ray Siemens, Jon Bath, Constance Crompton, Laura Estill, Tanja Niemann, Jon Saklofske, and Lynne Siemens, "An Open Social Scholarship Path for the Humanities," *Journal of Electronic Publishing* 25, no. 2 (2022): 6, https://doi.org/10.3998/jep.1973.
3   Jonathan P. Tennant, François Waldner, Damien C. Jacques, Paola Masuzzo, Lauren B. Collister, and Chris H. J. Hartgerink, "The Academic, Economic and Societal Impacts of Open Access: An Evidence-Based Review [Version 3; Peer Review: 4 Approved, 1 Approved with Reservations]," *F1000Research* 5 (2016): 3, art 632. https://doi.org/10.12688/f1000research.8460.3.
4   On the principle of common good, see Joan Wallach Scott, *Knowledge, Power, and Academic Freedom* (New York: Columbia University Press, 2019), 7. The history of OA reaches back to the fundamental concept of "knowledge as a commons, which is to say a shared resource," recognizing that "knowledge is never diminished with its use." Michael M. Crow and William B. Dabars, *The Fifth Wave: The Evolution of American Higher Education* (Baltimore: Johns Hopkins University Press, 2020), 193.
5   Arbuckle et al., "An Open Social Scholarship Path," 3.
6   See Marjorie Mayo, *Community-Based Learning and Social Movements* (Bristol: Policy Press, 2020). See also George Veletsianos and Royce Kimmons, "Networked Participatory Scholarship: Emergent Techno-Cultural Pressures toward Open and Digital Scholarship in Online Networks," *Computers and Education* 58, no. 2 (2012): 166–89, https://doi.org/10.1016/j.compedu.2011.10.001.

7 Eileen Scanlon, "Digital Scholarship: Identity, Interdisciplinarity, and Openness," *Frontiers in Digital Humanities* 5, no. 3 (2018), https://doi.org/10.3389/fdigh.2018.00003; Erin C. McKiernan, "Imagining the 'Open' University: Sharing Scholarship to Improve Research and Education," *PLOS Biology* 15, no. 10 (2017): e1002614, https://doi.org/10.1371/journal.pbio.1002614.

8 Open Scholarship Initiative, "Plan A," OSI's Plan A, April 20, 2020, https://plan-a.world/.

9 Peter Suber, *Open Access* (Cambridge, MA: MIT Press, 2012), chap. 1: "What Is Open Access," https://openaccesseks.mitpress.mit.edu/. See also John Willinsky, *The Access Principle: The Case for Open Access Research and Scholarship* (Cambridge, MA: MIT Press, 2006).

10 Charlotte Borgerud and Erik Borglund, "Open Research Data, an Archival Challenge?," *Archival Science*, no. 20 (2020): 279–302, https://doi.org/10.1007/s10502-020-09330-3. See also Danny Lämmerhirt, Ana Brandusescu, Natalia Domagala, and Patrick Enaholo, eds., *Situating Open Data: Global Trends in Local Contexts* (Cape Town: African Minds, 2020).

11 Ginny Barbour, "The Future of Academic Publishing: Disruption, Opportunity and a New Ecosystem," *Medical Journal of Australia* 211, no. 4 (2019): 151, https://doi.org/10.5694/mja2.50265.

12 Jonathan Tennant, Ritwik Agarwal, Ksenija Baždarić, David Brassard, Tom Crick, Daniel J. Dunleavy, Thomas Rhys Evans, Nicholas Gardner, Monica Gonzalez-Marquez, and Daniel Graziotin, "A Tale of Two 'Opens': Intersections between Free and Open Source Software and Open Scholarship," *SocArXiv*, March 6, 2020, 9, https://doi.org/10.31235/osf.io/2kxq8.

13 Victoria Martin, "The Concept of Openness in Scholarship," in *Open Praxis, Open Access: Digital Scholarship in Action*, ed. Darren Chase and Dana Haugh (Chicago: ALA Editions, 2020), 3–19.

14 The DARTS framework is set out in Glenn Hampson, Mel DeSart, Jason Steinhauer, Elizabeth A. Gadd, Lisa Janicke Hinchliffe, Micah Vandegrift, Chris Erdmann, and Rob Johnson, "OSI Policy Perspective 3: Open Science Roadmap Recommendations to UNESCO," *OSI Policy Perspectives, Open Scholarship Initiative*, June 2020, 27–8, https://doi.org/10.13021/osi2020.2735.

15 Arbuckle et al., "An Open Social Scholarship Path," 3. See also Mark D. Wilkinson, Michel Dumontier, and IJsbrand Jan Aalbersberg, "The FAIR Guiding Principles for Scientific Data Management and Stewardship," *Scientific Data* 3 (2016): art. 160018, https://doi.org/10.1038/sdata.2016.18.

16 This in turn is recasting academic responsibilities. As Ren observes, "The boundaries between academic publishing, scholarly communication and broader 'scholarship' are blurring, as a result of which, individual academics' roles and duties are being redefined." Xiang Ren, "The Quandary between Communication and

Certification: Individual Academics' Views on Open Access and Open Scholarship," *Online Information Review* 39, no. 5 (2015): 693, https://doi.org/10.1108/OIR-04-2015-0129.

17 Barbara Heinisc, Kristin Oswald, Maike Weißpflug, Sally Shuttleworth, and Geoffrey Belknap, "Citizen Humanities," in *The Science of Citizen Science*, ed. Katrin Vohland, Anne Land-Zandstra, Luigi Ceccaroni, Rob Lemmens, Josep Perelló, Marisa Ponti, Roeland Samson, and Katherin Wagenknecht (Cham, Switzerland: Springer, 2021), 97–118, https://doi.org/10.1007/978-3-030-58278-4_6. See also Daren C. Brabham, *Crowdsourcing* (Cambridge, MA: MIT Press, 2013); and Per Hetland, Palmyre Pierroux, and Line Esborg, eds., *A History of Participation in Museums and Archives: Traversing Citizen Science and Citizen Humanities* (London: Routledge, 2020).

18 See Alyssa Arbuckle, "Opportunities for Social Knowledge Creation in the Digital Humanities," in *Doing More Digital Humanities: Open Approaches to Creation, Growth, and Development*, ed. Constance Crompton, Richard J. Lane, and Ray Siemens (New York: Routledge, 2020), 290–300; Ben Showers, ed., *Library Analytics and Metrics: Using Data to Drive Decisions and Services* (London: Facet, 2015), 114–15.

19 See Thomas Eger and Marc Scheufen, *The Economics of Open Access: On the Future of Academic Publishing* (Cheltenham: Edward Elgar, 2018).

20 Jonathan Tennant, Neo Christopher Chung, and Tobias Steiner, "Major Socio-Cultural Barriers to Widespread Adoption of Open Scholarship," *SocArXiv*, April 6, 2020, https://doi.org/10.31235/osf.io/bth73.

21 Paul Longley Arthur, Lydia Hearn, Lucy Montgomery, Hugh Craig, Ray Siemens, and Alyssa Arbuckle, "Open Scholarship in Australia: A Review of Needs, Barriers and Opportunities," *Digital Scholarship in the Humanities* 36, no. 4 (2021): 795–812, https://doi.org/10.1093/llc/fqaa063.

22 Arbuckle et al., "An Open Social Scholarship Path," 1.

23 Ibid.

24 Elea Giménez Toledo, "Research Assessment in Humanities and Social Sciences in Review," *Revista Española de Documentación Científica* 41, no. 3 (2018): e208, https://doi.org/10.3989/redc.2018.3.1552; Nicolas Robinson-Garcia, Thed N. van Leeuwen, and Ismael Ràfols, "Using Altmetrics for Contextualised Mapping of Societal Impact: From Hits to Networks," *Science and Public Policy* 45, no. 6 (2018): 815–26, https://doi.org/10.1093/scipol/scy024.

25 Marcel Knöchelmann, "Open Science in the Humanities, or: Open Humanities?," *Publications* 7, no. 4 (2019): art. 65, https://doi.org/10.3390/publications7040065; Martin Paul Eve, "Open Access Publishing Models and How OA Can Work in the Humanities," *Bulletin of the Association for Information Science and Technology* 43, no. 5 (2017): 16–20, https://doi.org/10.1002/bul2.2017.1720430505; Jeremy L.

McLaughlin, "A New Open Humanities: Introduction," *Bulletin of the Association for Information Science and Technology* 43, no. 5 (2017): 12–15, https://doi.org/10.1002/bul2.2017.1720430504.

26 Peter Suber, "Why Is Open Access Moving So Slowly in the Humanities? (2004)," *American Philosophical Association (APA)* (blog), June 8, 2017, https://blog.apaonline.org/2017/06/08/open-access-in-the-humanities-part-2/.

1 Scholarly Communication from Past to Present

1 The mission of libraries has stayed the same for centuries, but "the way it is delivered is constantly evolving." Anja Oberländer and Torsten Reimer, eds., "Open Access and the Library," *Publications* 7, no. 1 (2019): 1, art. 3, https://doi.org/10.3390/publications7010003.

2 As Schnapp and Battles observe, "Few institutions have been more intimately associated in the collective mind with permanence, fixity, and the long-term preservation of knowledge than libraries." Jeffrey T. Schnapp and Matthew Battles, *The Library beyond the Book* (Cambridge, MA: Harvard University Press, 2014), 96.

3 Libraries reflect key eras in the development of information technology. Today online or digital libraries include assets that are born digital (created digitally) or digitalized (analog material digitized and made available electronically).

4 Wayne A. Wiegand, "Libraries and the Invention of Information," in *Companion to the History of the Book*, 2nd ed., ed. Jonathan Rose and Simon Eliot (Newark, NJ: John Wiley & Sons, 2019), 2:828; Eleanor Robson, "The Clay Tablet Book in Sumer, Assyria, and Babylonia," in *Companion to the History of the Book*, 2nd ed., ed. Jonathan Rose and Simon Eliot (Newark, NJ: John Wiley & Sons, 2019), 1:183–4.

5 Max Jakob Fölster, "Libraries and Archives in the Former Han Dynasty (206 BCE–9 CE): Arguing for a Distinction," in *Manuscripts and Archives: Comparative Views on Record-Keeping*, ed. Alessandro Bausi, Christian Brockmann, Michael Friedrich, and Sabine Kienitz (Berlin: De Gruyter, 2018), 201, https://doi.org/10.1515/9783110541397.

6 Hans Walter Gabler, "Textual Criticism," in *The Johns Hopkins Guide to Literary Theory and Criticism*, ed. Imre Szeman, Martin Kreiswirth, and Michael Groden, 2nd ed. (Baltimore: Johns Hopkins University Press, 2005), 901–8.

7 Scott Bennett, "Libraries and Learning: A History of Paradigm Change," *Portal: Libraries and the Academy* 9, no. 2 (2009): 181, https://doi.org/10.1353/pla.0.0049.

8 Construction of the library began in 1447. See Michael F. Suarez and H. R. Woudhuysen, eds., *The Oxford Companion to the Book* (Oxford: Oxford University Press, 2010), https://www.oxfordreference.com/view/10.1093/acref/9780198606

536.001.0001/acref-9780198606536-e-3025?rskey=gPTCVV&result=2965. See also https://en.unesco.org/silkroad/silk-road-themes/documentary-heritage/malatesta-novello-library.

9 William Eamon, "From the Secrets of Nature to Public Knowledge: The Origins of the Concept of Openness in Science," *Minerva* 23, no. 3 (1985): 321–47.
10 Ibid., 327–8.
11 David Banks, "Starting Science in the Vernacular: Notes on Some Early Issues of the *Philosophical Transactions* and the *Journal des Sçavans*, 1665–1700," *ASp: La Revue Du GERAS*, no. 55 (2009): 5–22, https://doi.org/10.4000/asp.213.
12 Eamon, "From the Secrets of Nature to Public Knowledge."
13 Melinda Baldwin, "Peer Review," *Encyclopedia of the History of Science*, January 2020, https://doi.org/10.34758/srde-jw27.
14 Henry Oldenburg, ed., "Introduction," *Philosophical Transactions of the Royal Society* 1, no. 1 (1665): 2.
15 See David A. Kronick, *A History of Scientific and Technical Periodicals: The Origins and Development of the Scientific and Technological Press, 1665–1790* (New York: Scarecrow Press, 1962).
16 Jonathan Tennant, Ritwik Agarwal, Ksenija Baždarić, David Brassard, Tom Crick, Daniel J. Dunleavy, Thomas Rhys Evans, Nicholas Gardner, Monica Gonzalez-Marquez, and Daniel Graziotin, "A Tale of Two 'Opens': Intersections between Free and Open Source Software and Open Scholarship," *SocArXiv*, March 6, 2020, 8, https://doi.org/10.31235/osf.io/2kxq8. See also Victoria Martin, "The Concept of Openness in Scholarship," in *Open Praxis, Open Access: Digital Scholarship in Action*, ed. Darren Chase and Dana Haugh (Chicago: ALA Editions, 2020); and Aileen Fyfe, Kelly Coate, Stephen Curry, Stuart Lawson, Noah Moxham, and Camilla Mørk Røstvik, "Untangling Academic Publishing: A History of the Relationship between Commercial Interests, Academic Prestige and the Circulation of Research" (Zenodo, May 2017), 5, https://doi.org/10.5281/zenodo.546100.
17 The full text of the Statute of Anne is available at https://avalon.law.yale.edu/18th_century/anne_1710.asp. For discussion, see John Willinsky, "When the Law Advances Access to Learning: Locke and the Origins of Modern Copyright," in *Reassembling Scholarly Communications: Histories, Infrastructures, and Global Politics of Open Access*, ed. Martin Paul Eve and Jonathan Gray (Cambridge, MA: MIT Press, 2020), 83–102, https://doi.org/10.7551/mitpress/11885.003.0011.
18 Ronan Deazley, *Rethinking Copyright: History, Theory, Language* (Cheltenham: Edward Elgar, 2006), 13–14.
19 Copyright law and protection remain highly complex and vary from country to country. See Nikos Koutras, *Building Equitable Access to Knowledge through Open Access Repositories* (Hershey, PA: IGI Global, 2019), chap. 2.
20 For discussion, see Bennett, "Libraries and Learning," 181–2.

21 Ibid., 181.
22 Rowland Lorimer, "Libraries, Scholars and Publishers in Digital Journal and Monograph Publishing," *Scholarly and Research Communication* 4, no. 1 (2013): 2, art. 010136, https://doi.org/10.22230/src.2013v4n1a43.
23 Fyfe et al., "Untangling Academic Publishing," 2.
24 Marvin Lazerson, "The Disappointments of Success: Higher Education after World War II," *Annals of the American Academy of Political and Social Science* 559 (The Changing Educational Quality of the Workforce) (September 1998): 64–76. For discussion of postwar funding for scientific research, see Mark W. Neff, "How Academic Science Gave Its Soul to the Publishing Industry," *Issues in Science and Technology* 36, no. 2 (2020): 35–43.
25 Vannevar Bush, *Science: The Endless Frontier* (Washington, DC: US Government Printing Office, 1945), https://www.nsf.gov/od/lpa/nsf50/vbush1945.htm.
26 Vannevar Bush, "As We May Think," *The Atlantic*, July 1945; Belinda Barnet, *Memory Machines: The Evolution of Hypertext* (London: Anthem Press, 2013), 11, 25, 31.
27 Fyfe et al., "Untangling Academic Publishing."
28 Neff, "How Academic Science Gave Its Soul to the Publishing Industry," 35.
29 Ibid., 35–6.
30 Ibid., 40. Brian Cox, "The Pergamon Phenomenon 1951–1991: Robert Maxwell and Scientific Publishing," *Learned Publishing* 15, no. 4 (2002): 273–4, https://doi.org/10.1087/095315102760319233.
31 Neff, "How Academic Science Gave Its Soul to the Publishing Industry," 39–41.
32 Fyfe et al., "Untangling Academic Publishing," 9.
33 Neff, "How Academic Science Gave Its Soul to the Publishing Industry," 41.
34 Francis Dodds, "The Changing Copyright Landscape in Academic Publishing," *Learned Publishing* 31, no. 3 (2018): 270, https://doi.org/10.1002/leap.1157.
35 Willinsky, "When the Law Advances Access."
36 Tennant et al., "A Tale of Two 'Opens,'" 6.
37 On the history of the Web, see https://timeline.web.cern.ch/cern-puts-world-wide-web-public-domain.
38 David Wiley and Cable Green, "Why Openness in Education?," in *Game Changers: Education and Information Technologies*, ed. Diana G. Oblinger (Boulder, CO: Educause, 2012), 82.
39 As Murphy and Costa write, "The web with its read and write features weakens the power of established gatekeepers—for example, publishers and academic journals of great renown and longstanding tradition—as it gives its users the autonomy to circumvent publishing conventions through self-publication practices." Mark Murphy and Cristina Costa, "Digital Scholarship, Higher Education and the Future

of the Public Intellectual," *Futures* 111 (2019): 208, https://doi.org/10.1016/j.futures.2018.04.011.

40 The established culture of team research in the sciences has provided opportunities for early-career researchers to contribute to research projects and be included in publication author lists. As noted by Milojevic, "Research teams are the fundamental social unit of science." Staša Milojević, "Principles of Scientific Research Team Formation and Evolution," *Proceedings of the National Academy of Sciences (PNAS)* 111, no. 11 (2014): 3984–9, https://doi.org/10.1073/pnas.1309723111.

41 Tennant et al., "A Tale of Two 'Opens,'" 27–8.

42 GNU is a recursive acronym standing for "GNU's Not Unix."

43 Richard Stallman, "The GNU Manifesto," GNU Operating System, 1985, https://www.gnu.org/gnu/manifesto.en.html. The GNU General Public License was released in 1989, and its underlying principles later led to the development of CC. See Tennant et al., "A Tale of Two 'Opens,'" 6–7. See also Rick Anderson, *Scholarly Communication: What Everyone Needs to Know* (Oxford: Oxford University Press, 2018), 104.

44 Richard Stallman, *Free Software, Free Society: Selected Essays of Richard M. Stallman* (Boston: GNU Press, 2002).

45 Tennant et al., "A Tale of Two 'Opens,'" 8.

46 Shao-Fang Wen, Mazaher Kianpour, and Basel Katt, "Security Knowledge Management in Open Source Software Communities," in *Innovative Security Solutions for Information Technology and Communications: SECITC 2018*, ed. J. L. Lanet and C. Toma, vol. 11359, Lecture Notes in Computer Science (Cham, Switzerland: Springer, 2019), https://doi.org/10.1007/978-3-030-12942-2_6.

47 Ginny Barbour and Scott Nicholls, "Open Access: Should One Model Ever Fit All?," *Australian Quarterly* 90, no. 3 (2019): 3–9. For a broader historical view, see Arwid Lund and Mariano Zukerfeld, *Corporate Capitalism's Use of Openness: Profit for Free?* (Cham, Switzerland: Palgrave Macmillan, 2020).

48 Alex Holzman, "US Open Access Publishing for the Humanities and Social Sciences," *European Political Science* 15, no. 2 (2016): 178, https://doi.org/10.1057/eps.2015.85.

49 See https://www.gutenberg.org/.

50 Fyfe et al., "Untangling Academic Publishing," 10.

51 For discussion, see Barbour and Nicholls, "Open Access," 4.

52 See https://pkp.sfu.ca/about/history/.

53 See https://www.openarchives.org/.

54 See https://creativecommons.org/about/.

55 Martin Paul Eve, *Open Access and the Humanities: Contexts, Controversies and the Future* (Cambridge: Cambridge University Press, 2014), 20.

56 Lawrence Lessig, *Free Culture: How Big Media Uses Technology and the Law to Lock Down Culture and Control Creativity* (New York: Penguin, 2004). Copyright infringement, unlike plagiarism, is not merely a breach of ethics; it is regarded as a criminal act in many countries.
57 Barbour and Nicholls, "Open Access," 5.
58 Ibid.
59 https://arxiv.org/.
60 See Christine L. Borgman, *Big Data, Little Data, No Data: Scholarship in the Networked World* (Cambridge, MA: MIT Press, 2015), 42–3.
61 Thomas Eger and Marc Scheufen, *The Economics of Open Access: On the Future of Academic Publishing* (Cheltenham: Edward Elgar, 2018), 14. "The problem is that that gold open access increases rather than reduces the cost of scholarly communication, and so confounds BOAI's expectation that open access will be more cost-effective." Richard Poynder, "Preface," in *Open Divide: Critical Studies on Open Access*, ed. Joachim Schöpfel and Ulrich Herb (Sacramento, CA: Library Juice Press, 2018), 3.
62 See Barbour and Nicholls, "Open Access," 5–6.
63 D. Mac Síthigh and J. Sheekey, "All That Glitters Is Not Gold, but Is It Diamond?," *SCRIPTed* 9, no. 3 (2012): 274–9, https://doi.org/10.2966/scrip.090312.274.
64 On the history and theory of the commons, see Charlotte Hess and Elinor Ostrom, eds., *Understanding Knowledge as a Commons: From Theory to Practice* (Cambridge, MA: MIT Press, 2007).
65 Zoé Ancion, Lidia Borrell-Damián, Pierre Mounier, Johan Rooryck, and Bregt Saenen, "Action Plan for Diamond Open Access" (Zenodo, March 2022), 3, https://doi.org/10.5281/zenodo.6282402.
66 For discussion, see Anderson, *Scholarly Communication*, 207–9.
67 Budapest Open Access Initiative, "Budapest Open Access Initiative," February 14, 2002, https://www.budapestopenaccessinitiative.org/read.
68 Boyer's concept of a renewed "scholarship of engagement" is a key reference point for the open scholarship movement. See Ernest L. Boyer, "The Scholarship of Engagement," *Bulletin of the American Academy of Arts and Sciences* 49, no. 7 (1996): 18–33, https://doi.org/10.2307/3824459. See also Eileen Scanlon, "Scholarship in the Digital Age: Open Educational Resources, Publication and Public Engagement," *British Journal of Educational Technology* 45, no. 1 (2014): 13, https://doi.org/10.1111/bjet.12010.
69 See Christopher Wilson, "Civil Society," in *The State of Open Data: Histories and Horizons*, ed. Tim Davies, Stephen B. Walker, Mor Rubinstein, and Fernando Perini (Cape Town: African Minds, 2019), 355–66. See also Murphy and Costa, "Digital Scholarship, Higher Education"; and Alyssa Arbuckle, Ray Siemens, Jon Bath, Constance Crompton, Laura Estill, Tanja Niemann, Jon Saklofske, and

Lynne Siemens, "An Open Social Scholarship Path for the Humanities," *Journal of Electronic Publishing* 25, no. 2 (2022): 12, https://doi.org/10.3998/jep.1973.

70 These are adapted from the five "Open Science schools of thought" formulated in Benedikt Fecher and Sascha Friesike, "Open Science: One Term, Five Schools of Thought," in *Opening Science: The Evolving Guide on How the Internet Is Changing Research, Collaboration and Scholarly Publishing*, ed. Sönke Bartling and Sascha Friesike (Cham, Switzerland: Springer, 2014), 17–47, https://doi.org/10.1007/978-3-319-00026-8_2. Tennant et al. consider "community and inclusion" to be a sixth driver (or "priority," as they refer to it). See section 5.6 of Jonathan Tennant, Jennifer Beamer, Jeroen Bosman, Björn Brembs, Neo Christopher Chung, Gail Clement, Tom Crick, Jonathan Dugan, Alastair Dunning, and David Eccles, "Foundations for Open Scholarship Strategy Development," *MetaArXiv*, January 30, 2019, https://doi.org/10.31222/osf.io/b4v8p.

71 Jessie Daniels and Polly Thistlethwaite, *Being a Scholar in the Digital Era: Transforming Scholarly Practice for the Public Good* (Bristol: Policy Press, 2016), 75; Martin, "The Concept of Openness"; Paul Longley Arthur and Lydia Hearn, "Toward Open Research: A Narrative Review of the Challenges and Opportunities for Open Humanities," *Journal of Communication* 71, no. 5 (2021): 827–53, https://doi.org/10.1093/joc/jqab028.

72 For a wide sample of topics, see Darren Chase and Dana Haugh, eds., *Open Praxis, Open Access: Digital Scholarship in Action* (Chicago: ALA Editions, 2020).

73 As aligned, for example, with the US Freedom of Information Act (1966) and the Electronic Freedom of Information Act Amendments (1996). See "The Freedom of Information Act, 5 U.S.C. § 552 as Amended by Public Law No. 110-175, 121 Stat. 2524" (2007), http://www.justice.gov/sites/default/files/oip/legacy/2014/07/23/amended-foia-redlined.pdf; "Electronic Freedom of Information Act Amendments of 1996 Public Law 1-4-238-Oct. 2, 1996" (1996), https://www.congress.gov/bill/104th-congress/house-bill/3802/text.

74 Murphy and Costa, "Digital Scholarship, Higher Education." See also Morag McDermont, Tim Cole, Janet Newman, and Angela Piccini, eds., *Imagining Regulation Differently: Co-Creating for Engagement* (Bristol: Policy Press, 2020). On OERs, see Rajiv S. Jhangiani and Robert Biswas-Diener, eds., *Open: The Philosophy and Practices That Are Revolutionizing Education and Science* (London: Ubiquity Press, 2017).

75 Erin C. McKiernan, "Imagining the 'Open' University: Sharing Scholarship to Improve Research and Education," *PLOS Biology* 15, no. 10 (2017): e1002614, https://doi.org/10.1371/journal.pbio.1002614.

2 Global Policies Promoting Openness

1. Budapest Open Access Initiative, "Budapest Open Access Initiative," February 14, 2002, https://www.budapestopenaccessinitiative.org/read; Bethesda Statement on Open Access Publishing, "Bethesda Statement on Open Access Publishing," June 20, 2003, https://dash.harvard.edu/bitstream/handle/1/4725199/Suber_bethesda.htm?sequence=3&isAllowed=y; Berlin Declaration on Open Access to Knowledge in the Sciences and Humanities, "Berlin Declaration on Open Access to Knowledge in the Sciences and Humanities," October 22, 2003, https://openaccess.mpg.de/Berlin-Declaration.
2. Budapest Open Access Initiative, "Budapest Open Access Initiative."
3. Ibid.
4. Herbert Van de Sompel and Carl Lagoze, "The Santa Fe Convention of the Open Archives Initiative," *D-Lib Magazine* 6, no. 2 (February 2000), http://www.dlib.org/dlib/february00/vandesompel-oai/02vandesompel-oai.html.
5. Gerry McKiernan, "E-Print Servers," *Science and Technology Libraries* 20, nos. 2–3 (2001): 149–58, https://doi.org/10.1300/J122v20n02_13.
6. Jean-Claude Guédon, "Open Access: Toward the Internet of the Mind," Budapest Open Access Initiative, 2017, https://www.budapestopenaccessinitiative.org/boai15/open-access-toward-the-internet-of-the-mind/.
7. Budapest Open Access Initiative, "Budapest Open Access Initiative."
8. Budapest Open Access Initiative, "Prologue: The Budapest Open Access Initiative after 10 Years," September 12, 2012, https://www.budapestopenaccessinitiative.org/boai10/.
9. Budapest Open Access Initiative, "Budapest Open Access Initiative: 20th Anniversary Recommendations," March 15, 2022, https://www.budapestopenaccessinitiative.org/boai20/.
10. Ibid.
11. Bethesda Statement on Open Access Publishing, "Bethesda Statement."
12. Ibid.
13. Berlin Declaration on Open Access to Knowledge in the Sciences and Humanities, "Berlin Declaration on Open Access."
14. Ibid.
15. For related discussion, see Agiatis Benardou, Erik Champion, Costis Dallas, and Lorna M. Hughes, eds., *Cultural Heritage Infrastructures in Digital Humanities* (London: Routledge, 2018).
16. Berlin Declaration on Open Access to Knowledge in the Sciences and Humanities, "Berlin Declaration on Open Access."
17. See https://openaccess.mpg.de/Berlin-Conferences.
18. https://okfn.org/.

19. *Declaration on Access to Research Data from Public Funding*, quoted in OECD, *OECD Principles and Guidelines for Access to Research Data from Public Funding* (Paris: OECD, 2007), 3, https://www.oecd.org/sti/inno/38500813.pdf.
20. Peter Murray-Rust, Cameron Neylon, Rufus Pollock, and John Wilbanks, "Panton Principles for Open Data in Science," February 19, 2010, http://pantonprinciples.okfn.org/.
21. Salvador Declaration on Open Access: The Developing World Perspective, "Salvador Declaration on Open Access: The Developing World Perspective," September 23, 2005, http://www.icml.org/public/documents/pdf/en/Dcl-Salvador-OpenAccess-en.pdf.
22. https://www.un.org/millenniumgoals/global.shtml. See in particular Target 8.F: "In cooperation with the private sector, make available benefits of new technologies, especially information and communications."
23. The Cape Town Open Education Declaration, "The Cape Town Open Education Declaration: Unlocking the Promise of Open Educational Resources," September 2007, https://www.capetowndeclaration.org/.
24. Open Government Partnership, "Open Government Declaration," September 2011, https://www.opengovpartnership.org/process/joining-ogp/open-government-declaration/.
25. Pisa Declaration on Policy Development for Grey Literature Resources, "Pisa Declaration on Policy Development for Grey Literature Resources," May 16, 2014, http://www.greynet.org/images/Pisa_Declaration,_May_2014.pdf.
26. San Francisco Declaration on Research Assessment, "San Francisco Declaration on Research Assessment," 2013, https://sfdora.org/read/.
27. Diana Hicks, Paul Wouters, Ludo Waltman, Sarah de Rijcke, and Ismael Rafols, "Leiden Manifesto for Research Metrics," 2015, http://www.leidenmanifesto.org/; Diana Hicks, Paul Wouters, Ludo Waltman, Sarah de Rijcke, and Ismael Rafols, "Bibliometrics: The Leiden Manifesto for Research Metrics," *Nature* 520, no. 7548 (2015): 429–31, https://doi.org/10.1038/520429a.
28. Peter Kraker, Daniel Dörler, Andreas Ferus, Robert Gutounig, Florian Heigl, Christian Kaier, Katharina Rieck, Elena Šimukovič, and Michela Vignoli, "Vienna Principles: A Vision for Scholarly Communication," 2016, https://viennaprinciples.org/.
29. Mark D. Wilkinson, Michel Dumontier, and IJsbrand Jan Aalbersberg, "The FAIR Guiding Principles for Scientific Data Management and Stewardship," *Scientific Data* 3 (2016): art. 160018, https://doi.org/10.1038/sdata.2016.18.
30. Ibid., 1.
31. Ibid.

32 G20 Summit, "G20 Leaders' Communique Hangzhou Summit," European Union, September 5, 2016, https://ec.europa.eu/commission/presscorner/detail/en/STATEMENT_16_2967.

33 Ministry of Education, Culture and Science, Government of the Netherlands, "Amsterdam Call for Action on Open Science," 2016, 2, https://www.government.nl/documents/reports/2016/04/04/amsterdam-call-for-action-on-open-science.

34 European Commission, Directorate-General for Communications Networks, Content and Technology, "European Cloud Initiative: Building a Competitive Data and Knowledge Economy in Europe—Document 52016DC0178" (Brussels: European Commission, April 19, 2016), https://eur-lex.europa.eu/legal-content/EN/TXT/?qid=1555074889405&uri=CELEX:52016DC0178.

35 European Science Foundation, "Plan S: Making Full and Immediate Open Access a Reality" (Brussels: European Commission and the European Research Council, 2018), https://www.coalition-s.org/.

36 The cOAlition S website states, "Although the Plan S principles refer to peer-reviewed scholarly publications, cOAlition S also strongly encourages that research data and other research outputs are made as open as possible and as closed as necessary. The early sharing of research results through preprints is also strongly encouraged." See Part II: Guidance on the Implementation of Plan S, Section 1—Aim and Scope, https://www.coalition-s.org/addendum-to-the-coalition-s-guidance-on-the-implementation-of-plan-s/principles-and-implementation/. For discussion, see Andros Tofield, "The cOAlition S and Plan S: Explained—European Legislation Requiring Scientific Publications Resulting from Research Funded by Public Grants Must Be Published in Compliant Open Access Journals or Platforms from 2020," *European Heart Journal* 40, no. 12 (2019): 952–3, https://doi.org/10.1093/eurheartj/ehz105.

37 "São Paulo Statement on Open Access: Joint Declaration by the African Open Science Platform, AmeliCA, cOAlition S, OA2020, and SciELO," May 1, 2019, https://www.coalition-s.org/wp-content/uploads/Sao-Paulo-Statement-OA-01052019.pdf.

38 CODATA (Committee on Data of the International Science Council), Simon Hodson, Barend Mons, Paul Uhlir, and Lili Zhang, "The Beijing Declaration on Research Data" (Zenodo, November 25, 2019), https://doi.org/10.5281/zenodo.3552329. See also European Commission, Directorate-General for Research and Innovation, *Future of Scholarly Publishing and Scholarly Communication: Report of the Expert Group to the European Commission* (Brussels: European Commission, January 2019), https://data.europa.eu/doi/10.2777/836532.

39 Ángel Borrego, Lluís Anglada, and Ernest Abadal, "Transformative Agreements: Do They Pave the Way to Open Access?," *Learned Publishing* 34, no. 2 (2021): 216–32, https://doi.org/10.1002/leap.1347.

40 Ibid.
41 Juan Pablo Alperin, "The Public Impact of Latin America's Approach to Open Access," Stanford University, 2015, http://purl.stanford.edu/jr256tk1194.
42 https://www.redalyc.org/.
43 http://amelica.org/index.php/en/home/.
44 https://www.lareferencia.info/en/.
45 Ginny Barbour and Scott Nicholls, "Open Access: Should One Model Ever Fit All?," *Australian Quarterly* 90, no. 3 (2019): 6.
46 Irina Bokova, director general of UNESCO, in David Souter, *Towards Inclusive Knowledge Societies: A Review of UNESCO's Action in Implementing the WSIS Outcomes* (Paris: UNESCO, 2010), 8.
47 Souter, *Towards Inclusive Knowledge Societies*, 11.
48 Ibid.
49 Maja Zalaznik, "We Cannot Have Peace without Education and Open Science," UNESCO, October 12, 2020, https://en.unesco.org/news/we-cannot-have-peace-without-education-and-open-science.
50 See https://www.unesco.org/en/communication-information/open-solutions/open-access-scientific-information/about.
51 https://www.unesco.org/en/communication-information/open-solutions/open-educational-resources.
52 https://goap.info/.
53 UNESCO, *UNESCO Recommendation on Open Science* (Paris: UNESCO, November 2021), https://unesdoc.unesco.org/ark:/48223/pf0000379949.locale=en.
54 Ibid., 6.
55 Ibid., 3.
56 Ibid., 7.
57 Marilyn Deegan and Kathryn Sutherland, *Transferred Illusions: Digital Technology and the Forms of Print* (Farnham: Ashgate, 2009), 99.
58 See Guédon, "Open Access," 19–20.
59 In 2013, for example, the Obama administration announced that all US agencies and departments supporting scientific research should make openly available published articles and data that result from public funding. See ibid., 20.
60 ORCID has become a key tool for open scholarship. See Sandra Fry, "Five Open Access Tips for 21st-Century Researchers: Tip #1," *QUT Library* (blog), October 21, 2019, https://blogs.qut.edu.au/library/2019/10/21/five-open-access-tips-for-21st-century-researchers-tip-1/.
61 Confederation of Open Access Repositories, "The Case for Interoperability for Open Access Repositories: Working Group 2—Repository Interoperability," July 8, 2011, 3. The text of the manifesto continues,

In order to create a seamless layer of content through connected repositories from around the world, Open Access relies on *interoperability*, the ability for systems to communicate with each other and pass information back and forth in a usable format. Interoperability allows us to exploit today's computational power so that we can aggregate, data mine, create new tools and services, and generate new knowledge from repository content.

62 See https://www.openaire.eu/.
63 Danny Kingsley, "Build It and They Will Come?: Support for Open Access in Australia," *Scholarly Research Communication* 4, no. 1 (2013): art. 010137, https://doi.org/10.22230/src.2013v4n1a39; Erin C. McKiernan, "Imagining the 'Open' University: Sharing Scholarship to Improve Research and Education," *PLOS Biology* 15, no. 10 (2017): e1002614, https://doi.org/10.1371/journal.pbio.1002614.

3 Barriers in Implementing Open Scholarship

1 Marianne Beaulieu, Mylaine Breton, Astrid Brousselle, and Fiona Harris, "Conceptualizing 20 Years of Engaged Scholarship: A Scoping Review," *PLOS ONE* 13, no. 2 (2018): e0193201, https://doi.org/10.1371/journal.pone.0193201.
2 On macro, micro, and meso actors, see Cameron Neylon, Rene Belsø, Magchiel Bijsterbosch, Bas Cordewener, Jérôme Foncel, Sascha Friesike, Aileen Fyfe, Neil Jacobs, Matthias Katerbow, Mikael Laakso, and Laurents Sesink, *Open Scholarship and the Need for Collective Action*, ed. Cameron Neylon (Zenodo, 2019), https://doi.org/10.5281/zenodo.3454688. For earlier discussion on the growing divide between "data rich" and "data poor," see William H. Dutton, "Reconfiguring Access in Research: Information, Expertise, and Experience," in *World Wide Research: Reshaping the Sciences and Humanities*, ed. William H. Dutton and Paul W. Jeffreys (Cambridge, MA: MIT Press, 2010), 27. These authors cite Steve Sawyer, "Data Wealth, Data Poverty, Science, and Cyberinfrastructure," *Prometheus* 26, no. 4 (2008): 355–71, https://doi.org/10.1080/08109020802459348.
3 Jennifer Rowsell, Ernest Morrell, and Donna E. Alvermann, "Confronting the Digital Divide: Debunking Brave New World Discourses," *Reading Teacher* 71, no. 2 (2017): 157–65, https://doi.org/10.1002/trtr.1603.
4 See Stefaan G. Verhulst and Andrew Young, *Open Data in Developing Economies: Toward Building an Evidence Base on What Works and How* (Cape Town: African Minds, 2017). See also Richard Poynder, "Preface," in *Open Divide: Critical Studies on Open Access*, ed. Joachim Schöpfel and Ulrich Herb (Sacramento, CA: Library Juice Press, 2018), 1–6.

5 United Nations General Assembly, "Universal Declaration of Human Rights," 217 (III) A (Paris, 1948), Article 27, https://www.un.org/en/about-us/universal-declaration-of-human-rights.
6 Numerous studies have reported such inequalities. For a recent study in the context of the United States, see Cynthia K. Sanders and Edward Scanlon, "The Digital Divide Is a Human Rights Issue: Advancing Social Inclusion through Social Work Advocacy," *Journal of Human Rights and Social Work*, no. 6 (2021): 130–43, https://doi.org/10.1007/s41134-020-00147-9.
7 Vincent Larivière, Stefanie Haustein, and Philippe Mongeon, "The Oligopoly of Academic Publishers in the Digital Era," *PLOS ONE* 10, no. 6 (2015): e0127502, https://doi.org/10.1371/journal.pone.0127502. The authors refer to analyses covering the period 1973–2013. See also Aileen Fyfe, Kelly Coate, Stephen Curry, Stuart Lawson, Noah Moxham, and Camilla Mørk Røstvik. "Untangling Academic Publishing: A History of the Relationship between Commercial Interests, Academic Prestige and the Circulation of Research" (Zenodo, May 2017), https://doi.org/10.5281/zenodo.546100.
8 Mandarin, Spanish, and Arabic are also other prominent languages. See Denisse Albornoz, Maggie Huang, Issra Martin, Maria Mateus, Aicha Touré, and Leslie Chan, "Framing Power: Tracing Key Discourses in Open Science Policies," in *ELPUB 2018* (Toronto, 2018), https://doi.org/10.4000/proceedings.elpub.2018.23; Leslie Chan, Barbara Kirsop, and Subbiah Arunachalam, "Towards Open and Equitable Access to Research and Knowledge for Development," *PLOS Medicine* 8, no. 3 (2011): e1001016, https://doi.org/10.1371/journal.pmed.1001016; Larivière, Haustein, and Mongeon, "Oligopoly of Academic Publishers."
9 Sci-Hub (https://sci-hub.hkvisa.net/), established in 2011, is a well-known online resource that offers access to millions of research publications at no cost, but it has been regularly accused of copyright infringement. For earlier discussion of challenges to copyright in the context of digital innovation, see Tarleton Gillespie, *Wired Shut: Copyright and the Shape of Digital Culture* (Cambridge, MA: MIT Press, 2007).
10 Albornoz et al., "Framing Power." For a historical perspective on open standards, see Andrew L. Russell, *Open Standards and the Digital Age: History, Ideology, and Networks* (New York: Cambridge University Press, 2014).
11 Paul Longley Arthur, Lydia Hearn, Lucy Montgomery, Hugh Craig, Ray Siemens, and Alyssa Arbuckle, "Open Scholarship in Australia: A Review of Needs, Barriers and Opportunities," *Digital Scholarship in the Humanities* 36, no. 4 (2021): 795–812, https://doi.org/10.1093/llc/fqaa063.
12 Wilhelm Peekhaus and Nicholas Proferes, "How Library and Information Science Faculty Perceive and Engage with Open Access," *Journal of Information Science* 41, no. 5 (2015): 640–61, https://doi.org/10.1177/0165551515587855; Stephen

Pinfield, "Making Open Access Work: The 'State-of-the-Art' in Providing Open Access to Scholarly Literature," *Online Information Review* 39, no. 5 (2015): 604–36, https://doi.org/10.1108/OIR-05-2015-0167; Jere Odell, Heather Coates, and Kristi Palmer, "Rewarding Open Access Scholarship in Promotion and Tenure: Driving Institutional Change," *College and Research Libraries News* 77, no. 7 (2016): 322–5, https://doi.org/10.5860/crln.77.7.9518.

13 Julia Gross and John Charles Ryan, "Landscapes of Research: Perceptions of Open Access (OA) Publishing in the Arts and Humanities," *Publications* 3, no. 2 (2015): 65–88, https://doi.org/10.3390/publications3020065; Peekhaus and Proferes, "How Library and Information Science Faculty Perceive and Engage with Open Access"; Pinfield, "Making Open Access Work"; Erin C. McKiernan, "Imagining the 'Open' University: Sharing Scholarship to Improve Research and Education," *PLOS Biology* 15, no. 10 (2017): e1002614, https://doi.org/10.1371/journal.pbio.1002614; Juliana Elisa Raffaghelli, "Exploring the (Missed) Connections between Digital Scholarship and Faculty Development: A Conceptual Analysis," *International Journal of Educational Technology in Higher Education*, no. 14 (2017): art. 20, https://doi.org/10.1186/s41239-017-0058-x; Bhuva Narayan, Edward J. Luca, Belinda Tiffen, Ashley England, Mal Booth, and Henry Boateng, "Scholarly Communication Practices in Humanities and Social Sciences: A Study of Researchers' Attitudes and Awareness of Open Access," *Open Information Science* 2, no. 1 (2018): 168–80, https://doi.org/10.1515/opis-2018-0013.

14 Julia E. Rodriguez, "Awareness and Attitudes about Open Access Publishing: A Glance at Generational Differences," *Journal of Academic Librarianship* 40, no. 6 (2014): 604–10, https://doi.org/10.1016/j.acalib.2014.07.013; Narayan et al., "Scholarly Communication Practices in Humanities and Social Sciences"; Raffaghelli, "Exploring the (Missed) Connections"; Gross and Ryan, "Landscapes of Research."

15 Beaulieu et al., "Conceptualizing 20 Years of Engaged Scholarship." Beaulieu et al. write about the institutional-level logistical arrangements necessary for engaged scholarship (p. 12).

16 On generational approaches to publication strategy, see Björn Hammarfelt and Sarah de Rijcke, "Accountability in Context: Effects of Research Evaluation Systems on Publication Practices, Disciplinary Norms, and Individual Working Routines in the Faculty of Arts at Uppsala University," *Research Evaluation* 24, no. 1 (2015): 75, https://doi.org/10.1093/reseval/rvu029.

17 Juan P. Alperin, Carol Muñoz Nieves, Lesley A. Schimanski, Gustavo E. Fischman, Meredith T. Niles, and Erin C. McKiernan, "Meta-Research: How Significant Are the Public Dimensions of Faculty Work in Review, Promotion and Tenure Documents?," *eLife*, no. 8 (2019): e42254, https://doi.org/10.7554/eLife.42254.001; Samuel Moore, Cameron Neylon, Martin Paul Eve, Daniel Paul O'Donnell, and

Damian Pattinson, "'Excellence R Us': University Research and the Fetishisation of Excellence," *Palgrave Communications* 1, no. 3 (2017): art. 16105, https://doi.org/10.1057/palcomms.2016.105.

18. Beaulieu et al., "Conceptualizing 20 Years of Engaged Scholarship."
19. Standards and solutions for digital preservation include those developed by the Open Preservation Foundation (established 2010). See https://openpreservation.org/.
20. Martin Borchert, Andrew Harrison, Andrew Heath, Belinda Tiffen, Janet Fletcher, Katrina Dewis, Maude Frances, Virginia Barbour, and Natasha Simons, *CAUL Fair, Affordable and Open Access to Knowledge Program: CAUL Review of Australian Repository Infrastructure*, Council of Australian University Librarians (CAUL), Australian Policy Online, March 15, 2019, https://apo.org.au/node/243791.
21. McKiernan, "Imagining the 'Open' University," 14; Cameron Neylon, "As a Researcher … I'm a Bit Bloody Fed Up with Data Management," *Science in the Open* (blog), June 16, 2017, https://cameronneylon.net/blog/as-a-researcher-im-a-bit-bloody-fed-up-with-data-management/.
22. External hosting is often used for projects that require additional services, such as app development or other platforms used to engage with the public. Yet a major drawback can be that once project funding is expended, domain licenses and hosting arrangements may expire, and the online data may not be maintained or preserved.
23. Jean-Claude Guédon, "Open Access: Toward the Internet of the Mind," Budapest Open Access Initiative, 2017, 16, https://www.budapestopenaccessinitiative.org/boai15/open-access-toward-the-internet-of-the-mind/.
24. Jill Benn and Martin Borchert, "F.A.I.R. Is Fair for Research: Australian Initiatives to Improve Openness in the Scholarly Communications Environment," in *Proceedings of the IATUL Conferences* (Purdue University, Purdue e-Pubs, 2018). Few librarians have the time or incentives to maintain accessible platforms for unpublished materials such as datasets, primary materials, digitized collections, images, and multimedia. Yet repositories can effectively offer "an accessible locus for unreviewed materials, including local conferences, data sets, primary source materials, and the like." Alex Holzman, "US Open Access Publishing for the Humanities and Social Sciences," *European Political Science* 15, no. 2 (2016): 179, https://doi.org/10.1057/eps.2015.85.
25. Guédon, "Open Access," 24.
26. Jessica Clemons, "Open Science and Open Data: What Can We Learn from the Open Access Movement?," in *Open Praxis, Open Access: Digital Scholarship in Action*, ed. Darren Chase and Dana Haugh (Chicago: ALA Editions, 2020), 212.
27. Changes to the UK Copyright Act in 1988 meant that while authors continued to have exclusive rights to reproduce, adapt, display, and distribute their work, others

could now copy, distribute, and create derivative works in limited ways, without having to gain permission, under the law of "fair dealing." See Copyright, Designs and Patents Act 1988 (c. 48), United Kingdom, 1988, https://www.legislation.gov.uk/ukpga/1988/48/enacted. Similar legislation was introduced in the EU and other jurisdictions.

28 Rick Anderson, *Scholarly Communication: What Everyone Needs to Know* (Oxford: Oxford University Press, 2018), 90–3.

29 McKiernan, "Imagining the 'Open' University."

30 See Hannah Lewi, Wally Smith, Dirk vom Lehn, and Steven Cooke, eds., *The Routledge International Handbook of New Digital Practices in Galleries, Libraries, Archives, Museums and Heritage Sites* (Abingdon: Routledge, 2020). See also Stefan Buddenbohm, Nathanael Cretin, Elly Dijk, Bertrand Gaiffe, Maaike de Jong, Jean-Luc Minel, and Nathalie Le Tellier-Becquart, "State of the Art Report on Open Access Publishing of Research Data in the Humanities," DARIAH, 2016, 13, https://halshs.archives-ouvertes.fr/halshs-01357208v3.

4 Toward the Open Humanities

1 The first use of the term *open science* in relation to the principles now widely associated with the concept is often traced to Daryl E. Chubin, "Open Science and Closed Science: Tradeoffs in a Democracy," *Science, Technology, & Human Values* 10, no. 2 (1985): 73–81.

2 Sarah E. Ali-Khan, Antoine Jean, and E. Richard Gold, "Identifying the Challenges in Implementing Open Science [Version 1; Peer Review: 2 Approved]," *MNI Open Research* 2, no. 5 (October 12, 2018): 3, https://doi.org/10.12688/MNIOPENRES.12805.1.

3 See the seven-point agenda set out in Tibor Koltay, "Quality of Open Research Data: Values, Convergences and Governance," *Information* 11, no. 4 (2020): 175, https://doi.org/10.3390/info11040175; Tobias Dienlin, Niklas Johannes, Nicholas David Bowman, Philipp K. Masur, Sven Engesser, Anna Sophie Kümpel, Josephine Lukito, Lindsey M. Bier, Renwen Zhang, Benjamin K. Johnson, Richard Huskey, Frank M. Schneider, Johannes Breuer, Douglas A. Parry, Ivar Vermeulen, Jacob T. Fisher, Jaime Banks, René Weber, David A. Ellis, Tim Smits, James D. Ivory, Sabine Trepte, Bree McEwan, Eike Mark Rinke, German Neubaum, Stephan Winter, Christopher J. Carpenter, Nicole Krämer, Sonja Utz, Julian Unkel, Xiaohui Wang, Brittany I. Davidson, Nuri Kim, Andrea Stevenson Won, Emese Domahidi, Neil A. Lewis, and Claes de Vreese, "An Agenda for Open Science in Communication," *Journal of Communication* 71, no. 1 (2020): 1–26, https://doi.org/10.1093/joc/jqz052.

4 UNESCO, *UNESCO Recommendation on Open Science* (Paris: UNESCO, November 2021), section II, subsection 6, https://unesdoc.unesco.org/ark:/48223/pf0000379 949.locale=en.
5 Dienlin et al., "An Agenda for Open Science."
6 Martin Paul Eve, ed., *Open Access and the Humanities: Contexts, Controversies and the Future* (Cambridge: Cambridge University Press, 2014); Peter Suber, "Why Is Open Access Moving So Slowly in the Humanities? (2004)," *American Philosophical Association (APA)* (blog), June 8, 2017, https://blog.apaonline.org/2017/06/08/open-access-in-the-humanities-part-2/.
7 Suber, "Why Is Open Access Moving So Slowly in the Humanities?"; Eve, *Open Access and the Humanities*.
8 Eric Johnson, "On a Definition of 'Open Humanities,'" *Eric D. M. Johnson* (blog), April 2, 2012, https://www.ericdmjohnson.com/2012/04/02/on-a-definit ion-of-open-humanities/.
9 Snow writes, "I believe the intellectual life of the whole of western society is increasingly being split into two polar groups. ... Literary intellectuals at one pole—at the other scientists. ... Between the two a gulf of mutual incomprehension." Charles Percy Snow, *The Two Cultures and the Scientific Revolution* (London: Cambridge University Press, 1959), 2, https://doi.org/10.2307/1578601.
10 Dienlin et al., "An Agenda for Open Science."
11 Sotirios Sarantakos, *Social Research* (Melbourne: Macmillan, 1993).
12 Snow, *The Two Cultures*; Sarantakos, *Social Research*.
13 Marcel Knöchelmann, "Open Science in the Humanities, or: Open Humanities?," *Publications* 7, no. 4 (2019): art. 65, https://doi.org/10.3390/publications7040065. Knöchelmann argues that this issue relates to humanities' practice rather than to licensing: "It is in the humanities where the nuances of argument and expression matter. Both these issues are much less present in disciplines of the sciences."
14 Ibid.; Sarantakos, *Social Research*.
15 Michel Foucault, *Power/Knowledge: Selected Interviews and Other Writings, 1972–1977 by Michel Foucault*, ed. Colin Gordon, trans. Colin Gordon, Leo Marshall, John Mepham, and Kate Soper (New York: Pantheon Books, 1980), 106–7.
16 Snow, *The Two Cultures*.
17 Knöchelmann, "Open Science in the Humanities."
18 A case in point is the heavy metal band Metallica, which sued the music file-sharing platform Napster and many universities for copyright infringement, arguing that using university servers to provide students with free access to their music violated the law. This example led to international conventions calling for removal of economic barriers to peer sharing of data. See discussion in Nikos Koutras, *Building Equitable Access to Knowledge through Open Access Repositories* (Hershey, PA: IGI Global, 2019), 12.

19 Martin Paul Eve, "Open Access Publishing Models and How OA Can Work in the Humanities," *Bulletin of the Association for Information Science and Technology* 43, no. 5 (2017): 16–20, https://doi.org/10.1002/bul2.2017.1720430505; Anna Severin, Matthias Egger, Martin Paul Eve, and Daniel Hürlimann, "Discipline-Specific Open Access Publishing Practices and Barriers to Change: An Evidence-Based Review [Version 2; Peer Review: 2 Approved, 1 Approved with Reservations]," *F1000Research* 7 (2020): art. 1925, https://doi.org/10.12688/f1000research.17328.2.

20 Bhuva Narayan, Edward J. Luca, Belinda Tiffen, Ashley England, Mal Booth, and Henry Boateng, "Scholarly Communication Practices in Humanities and Social Sciences: A Study of Researchers' Attitudes and Awareness of Open Access," *Open Information Science* 2, no. 1 (2018): 168–80, https://doi.org/10.1515/opis-2018-0013.

21 Peter Suber, "Preface," in *Open Access and the Humanities: Contexts, Controversies and the Future*, ed. Martin Paul Eve (Cambridge: Cambridge University Press, 2014), ix–xi. As Suber writes,

> Journal articles tend to be primary literature in the sciences and secondary literature in the humanities. In the sciences, books tend to synthesise research published in articles, while in the humanities articles tend to report on the history and interpretation of books. Tenure in the sciences depends more on published articles than on books, while tenure in the humanities depends more on published books than on articles. (x)

See also Jere Odell, Heather Coates, and Kristi Palmer, "Rewarding Open Access Scholarship in Promotion and Tenure: Driving Institutional Change," *College and Research Libraries News* 77, no. 7 (2016): 322–5, https://doi.org/10.5860/crln.77.7.9518.

22 Eve, "Open Access Publishing Models."

23 Steffen Lemke, Maryam Mehrazar, Athanasios Mazarakis, and Isabella Peters, "'When You Use Social Media You Are Not Working': Barriers for the Use of Metrics in Social Sciences," *Frontiers in Research Metrics and Analytics* 3, no. 39 (2019), https://doi.org/10.3389/frma.2018.00039; Elea Giménez Toledo, "Research Assessment in Humanities and Social Sciences in Review," *Revista Española de Documentación Científica* 41, no. 3 (2018): e208, https://doi.org/10.3989/redc.2018.3.1552.

24 Toledo, "Research Assessment in Humanities," 8:

> The diversity in research and publishing within the Humanities and the Social Sciences is and will be a crucial factor in the evaluation of these fields. Since they generate a less monolithic knowledge than the positive sciences, the patterns and publication channels are more diverse, and this has implications in scientific evaluation: it requires more complete sources

that provide information on the wide range of journals, publishers and other communication channels. These sources should combine the diversity and plurality in research topics, languages or methodologies with the quality and/or rigor in the selection of the texts that are published. Precisely because publication channels in these fields are far more numerous and because it is necessary to distinguish the more consistent research and the more selective channels, the development of objective indicators providing additional information is fundamental.

25 Björn Hammarfelt and Gaby Haddow, "Conflicting Measures and Values: How Humanities Scholars in Australia and Sweden Use and React to Bibliometric Indicators," *Journal of the Association for Information Science and Technology* 69, no. 7 (2018): 924–35, https://doi.org/10.1002/asi.24043.
26 Björn Hammarfelt, "Four Claims on Research Assessment and Metric Use in the Humanities," *Bulletin of the Association for Information Science and Technology* 43, no. 5 (2017): 33–8, https://doi.org/10.1002/bul2.2017.1720430508. Regarding audiences, Hammarfelt writes,

> Citation analysis demands that the intended audience is rather narrow, but the audience of humanities research is quite diverse and not easily demarcated. Nederhof distinguishes three major audiences: international scholars, national scholars and a lay audience with professionals (for example journalists, librarians, archivists, etc.) being seen as a possible fourth audience. Only the first audience—international scholars—is represented in major citation databases such as Web of Science and Scopus, and even for this group the coverage is low. While extending the databases might lead to greater coverage, important groups (the public and professionals) are still omitted.
>
> The heterogeneous audience for the humanities suggests that researchers potentially have a broad reach, including an audience outside the academy, which means that in some humanities fields recognition from peers is not the only way of building reputation. This diversity gives scholars in the humanities a considerable degree of freedom when choosing research topics, but at the same time it limits the possibility of attracting citations. (35–6)

27 Foucault, *Power/Knowledge*, 107.
28 Ibid., 81.
29 Toledo, "Research Assessment in Humanities," 3–4.
30 See Melissa C. Márquez and Ana Maria Porras, "Science Communication in Multiple Languages Is Critical to Its Effectiveness," *Frontiers in Communication* 5 (2020), https://doi.org/10.3389/fcomm.2020.00031.

31 Pierre Mounier, "'Publication Favela' or Bibliodiversity?: Open Access Publishing Viewed from a European Perspective," *Learned Publishing* 31, no. S1 (2018): 299–305, https://doi.org/10.1002/leap.1194.

32 Wilhelm Peekhaus and Nicholas Proferes, "How Library and Information Science Faculty Perceive and Engage with Open Access," *Journal of Information Science* 41, no. 5 (2015): 640–61, https://doi.org/10.1177/0165551515587855.

33 Steven Laporte, "Preprint for the Humanities: Fiction or a Real Possibility?," *Studia Historiae Scientiarum* 16 (2017): 367–78, https://doi.org/10.4467/2543702X SHS.17.014.7715.

34 Narayan et al., "Scholarly Communication Practices in Humanities and Social Sciences"; Carol Tenopir, Kenneth Levine, Suzie Allard, Lisa Christian, Rachel Volentine, Reid Boehm, Frances Nichols, David Nicholas, Hamid R. Jamali, Eti Herman, and Anthony Watkinson, "Trustworthiness and Authority of Scholarly Information in a Digital Age: Results of an International Questionnaire," *Journal of the Association for Information Science and Technology* 67, no. 10 (2016): 2344–61, https://doi.org/10.1002/asi.23598.

35 Clifford Lynch, "Guest Editorial: Updating the Agenda for Academic Libraries and Scholarly Communications," *College and Research Libraries* 78, no. 2 (2017): 126, https://doi.org/10.5860/crl.78.2.126.

36 Hammarfelt and Haddow, "Conflicting Measures and Values"; Michael Ochsner, Sven E. Hug, and Hans-Dieter Daniel, "Humanities Scholars' Conceptions of Research Quality," in *Research Assessment in the Humanities: Towards Criteria and Procedures*, ed. Michael Ochsner, Sven E. Hug, and Hans-Dieter Daniel (Cham, Switzerland: Springer, 2016), 43–69, https://doi.org/10.1007/978-3-319-29016-4_5.

37 While monographs remain preeminent in the humanities, some have argued that this long-established form is becoming outdated and no longer viable. See, for example, Kathleen Fitzpatrick, *Planned Obsolescence: Publishing, Technology, and the Future of the Academy* (New York: New York University Press, 2011), 4.

38 Eve, "Open Access Publishing Models," 16.

39 The Australian database Trove was recently described as Australia's "digital memory." Kelly Burke, "Trove: National Library of Australia's Digital Archives Thrown $33m Lifeline by Federal Government," *Guardian*, April 3, 2023, Australia edition, https://www.theguardian.com/books/2023/apr/03/trove-national-library-of-australias-digital-archives-thrown-33m-lifeline-by-federal-government.

40 Maciej Maryl, Tito Orlandi, Bernard Rentier, and Eveline Wandl-Vogt, "Sustainable and FAIR Data Sharing in the Humanities," *Recommendations of the ALLEA Working Group E-Humanities* (Berlin: ALLEA All European Academies, February 2020), https://doi.org/10.7486/DRI.tq582c863; Stefan Buddenbohm, Nathanael Cretin, Elly Dijk, Bertrand Gaiffe, Maaike de Jong, Jean-Luc Minel, and Nathalie Le Tellier-Becquart, "State of the Art Report on Open Access Publishing of Research

Data in the Humanities" (DARIAH, 2016), https://halshs.archives-ouvertes.fr/halshs-01357208v3; Charlotte Borgerud and Erik Borglund, "Open Research Data, An Archival Challenge?," *Archival Science*, no. 20 (2020): 279–302, https://doi.org/10.1007/s10502-020-09330-3.

41 Alyssa Arbuckle, Ray Siemens, Jon Bath, Constance Crompton, Laura Estill, Tanja Niemann, Jon Saklofske, and Lynne Siemens, "An Open Social Scholarship Path for the Humanities," *Journal of Electronic Publishing* 25, no. 2 (2022): 5, https://doi.org/10.3998/jep.1973; Muriel Swijghuisen Reigersberg, "Problematizing Digital Research Evaluation Using DOIs in Practice-Based Arts, Humanities and Social Science Research [Version 1; Peer Review: 2 Approved]," *F1000Research* 4 (2015): 3–4, art. 193, https://doi.org/10.12688/f1000research.6506.1. For Borgman, "recognizing that some phenomena could be treated as data is itself a scholarly act." Christine L. Borgman, *Big Data, Little Data, No Data: Scholarship in the Networked World* (Cambridge, MA: MIT Press, 2015), 5.

42 Erzsébet Tóth-Czifra, "The Risk of Losing the *Thick Description*: Data Management Challenges Faced by the Arts and Humanities in the Evolving FAIR Data Ecosystem," in *Digital Technology and the Practices of Humanities Research*, ed. Jennifer Edmond (Cambridge: Open Book, 2019), 235–66, https://doi.org/10.11647/obp.0192.10.

43 Costis Dallas, Nephelie Chatzidaiakou, Agiatis Benardou, Michael Bender, Aurélien Berra, Claire Clivaz, John Cunningham, Meredith Dabek, Patricia Garrido, Elena Gonzalez-Blanco, Jurij Hadalin, Lorna Hughes, Beat Immenhauser, Anne Joly, Ingrida Kelpšienė, Michał Kozak, Koraljka Kuzman, Marko Lukin, Irena Marinski, Maciej Maryl, Robert Owain, Eliza Papaki, Gerlinde Schneider, Walter Scholger, Susan Schreibman, Zoe Schubert, Toma Tasovac, Manfred Thaller, Piotr Wciślik, Marcin Werla, and Tvrtko Zebec, "European Survey on Scholarly Practices and Digital Needs in the Arts and Humanities: Survey Highlights," in *Digital Methods and Practices Observatory Working Group (DiMPO) DARIAH-EU European Research Infrastructure Consortium* (DARIAH-EU, October 2016).

44 Erin C. McKiernan, "Imagining the 'Open' University: Sharing Scholarship to Improve Research and Education," *PLOS Biology* 15, no. 10 (2017): e1002614, https://doi.org/10.1371/journal.pbio.1002614; George Veletsianos and Royce Kimmons, "Networked Participatory Scholarship: Emergent Techno-Cultural Pressures toward Open and Digital Scholarship in Online Networks," *Computers and Education* 58, no. 2 (2012): 166–89, https://doi.org/10.1016/j.compedu.2011.10.001.

45 Jean-Claude Burgelman, Corina Pascu, Katarzyna Szkuta, Rene Von Schomberg, Athanasios Karalopoulos, Konstantinos Repanas, and Michel Schouppe, "Open Science, Open Data, and Open Scholarship: European Policies to Make Science

Fit for the Twenty-First Century," *Frontiers in Big Data* 2 (2019): 43, https://doi.org/10.3389/fdata.2019.00043.

46 Melissa Terras, "Opening Access to Collections: The Making and Using of Open Digitised Cultural Content," *Online Information Review* [Special Issue on "Open Access: Redrawing the Landscape of Scholarly Communication," ed. G. E. Gorman and J. Rowley] 39, no. 5 (2015): 733–52, https://doi.org/10.1108/OIR-06-2015-0193.

47 Koutras, *Building Equitable Access to Knowledge*, 144–5.

48 Borgerud and Borglund, "Open Research Data."

49 Sandra Collins, Natalie Harrower, Dag Trygve Truslew Haug, Beat Immenhauser, Gerhard Lauer, Tito Orlandi, Laurent Romary, and Eveline Wandl-Vogt, *Going Digital: Creating Change in the Humanities* (Berlin: ALLEA All European Academies, 2015), https://www.allea.org/wp-content/uploads/2015/07/Going-Digital_digital-version.pdf; Maryl et al., "Sustainable and FAIR."

50 Maryl et al., "Sustainable and FAIR."

51 Research Data Alliance International Indigenous Data Sovereignty Interest Group, "CARE Principles for Indigenous Data Governance" (The Global Indigenous Data Alliance, September 2019), https://www.gida-global.org/care. For discussion, see Stephanie Russo Carroll, Ibrahim Garba, Oscar L. Figueroa-Rodríguez, Jarita Holbrook, Raymond Lovett, Simeon Materechera, Mark Parsons, Kay Raseroka, Desi Rodriguez-Lonebear, Robyn Rowe, Rodrigo Sara, Jennifer D. Walker, Jane Anderson, and Maui Hudson, "The CARE Principles for Indigenous Data Governance," *Data Science Journal* 19, no. 1 (2020): art. 43, https://doi.org/10.5334/dsj-2020-043. See also Maggie Walter, Tahu Kukutai, Stephanie Russo Carroll, and Desi Rodriguez-Lonebear, eds., *Indigenous Data Sovereignty and Policy* (Abingdon, Oxon: Routledge, 2021). A set of principles relating to data sovereignty in Aotearoa New Zealand published just prior to the formulation of the CARE principles is an example of how such values can be adapted in a national context. See Te Mana Raraunga—Māori Data Sovereignty Network, "Principles of Māori Data Sovereignty," October 2018, https://www.temanararaunga.maori.nz/s/TMR-Maori-Data-Sovereignty-Principles-Oct-2018.pdf.

52 We have learned from the international history of colonization, for example, the catastrophic consequences of cutting people off from their cultural heritage or denying its value, as has occurred with First Nations Australians since European settlement.

53 With the sudden demise of traditional letter writing in the age of social media, for example, personal letters will have increased cultural value as historical data. Similarly, stories, visual art, music, and dance can provide important data about cultural identity and social change.

54 Infrastructure can also be localized. For example, an institutional repository may function as the key infrastructure for a particular organization.

55 G. Bilder, J. Lin, and C. Neylon, "The Principles of Open Scholarly Infrastructure," 2020, https://doi.org/10.24343/C34W2H. "First developed in a 2015 blog post, POSI offers a set of guidelines by which open scholarly infrastructure organisations and initiatives that support the research community can be run and sustained." https://openscholarlyinfrastructure.org/about.
56 Bilder, Lin, and Neylon, https://openscholarlyinfrastructure.org/faq/.
57 See, for example, discussion in Paul Longley Arthur, "Tracing the Development of Digital Humanities in Australia," in *Digital Humanities and Scholarly Research Trends in the Asia-Pacific*, ed. Shun-han Rebekah Wong, Haipeng Li, and Min Chou (Hershey, PA: IGI Global, 2019), 2–3, https://doi.org/10.4018/978-1-5225-7195-7.ch001.
58 https://www.clarin.eu/.
59 https://www.dariah.eu/.
60 https://www.europeana.eu/en. An initiative of the European Union, this web portal enables exploration of digitized heritage collections across Europe.
61 https://www.e-rihs.eu/. E-RIHS provides expertise, data, and technologies to standardize the interpretation, safeguarding, documentation, and management of cultural heritage data.
62 https://www.openaire.eu/. OpenAIRE is assisting researchers to meet the mandates of funding agencies and governments to make their research open and accessible.
63 https://operas-eu.org/. OPERAS is systematically integrating books, monographs, and humanities data into the European Open Science Cloud.
64 See Patrik Svensson, "The Humanistiscope: Exploring the Situatedness of Humanities Infrastructure," in *Between Humanities and the Digital*, ed. Patrik Svensson and David Theo Goldberg (Cambridge, MA: MIT Press, 2015), 337–53.
65 https://hcommons.org/.
66 The Rijksmuseum has been a leader in the museum sector, providing digital images of objects from its collection and descriptive object information and bibliographic data without restrictions on reuse. https://www.rijksmuseum.nl/en.
67 https://www.timemachine.eu/.
68 See, for example, the in-progress Hanyang Time Machine project in South Korea. http://dh.aks.ac.kr/~my9univ/image/KADH2021/S1/Hanyang_TimeMachine_Overview.pdf.
69 https://hsscommons.ca/.
70 https://sadilar.org/. Funded by the Department of Science and Innovation (DSI) of the government of South Africa, SADiLaR forms part of the broader DSI South African Research Infrastructure Roadmap (SARIR) Programme.
71 https://iitikship.iiti.ac.in/.
72 https://iitikship.iiti.ac.in/site/about/.
73 https://www.paradisec.org.au/.

74 https://tlcmap.org/.
75 https://ardc.edu.au/program/hass-rdc-indigenous-research-capability/.
76 https://www.austlit.edu.au/. Austlist uses an institutional subscription model.
77 https://www.ausstage.edu.au/.
78 https://www.daao.org.au/.
79 https://huni.net.au/. An innovative example of an infrastructure that connects cultural collections and enables social scholarship, HuNI was funded by the National eResearch Collaboration Tools and Resources initiative of the Australian Government.
80 Okune et al. advocate "inclusive knowledge infrastructures," which can be "defined as the tools, platforms, networks and other socio-technical mechanisms that deliberately allow for multiple forms of participation amongst a diverse set of actors, and which purposefully acknowledge and seek to redress power relations within a given context." Angela Okune, Rebecca Hillyer, Leslie Chan, Denisse Albornoz, and Alejandro Posada, "Whose Infrastructure?: Towards Inclusive and Collaborative Knowledge Infrastructures in Open Science," in *Connecting the Knowledge Commons: From Projects to Sustainable Infrastructure*, ed. Leslie Chan and Pierre Mounier (Marseille: OpenEdition Books, 2019), https://books.openedition.org/oep/9072. There are choices, for example, around what to accept, describe, catalogue, and document. See Melissa Terras, "Opening Access to Collections."
81 The field of critical infrastructure studies is contributing significant insights into social and political dimensions of infrastructure design. See https://cistudies.org/.
82 Martin Rees, "A Longitude Prize for the Twenty-First Century," *Nature* 509, no. 7501 (2014): 401, https://doi.org/10.1038/509401a. See also William J. H. Andrewes and Dava Sobel, *Longitude: The True Story of a Lone Genius Who Solved the Greatest Scientific Problem of His Time* (London: Fourth Estate, 1999).
83 Yin Liu, "Appeal to the Public: Lessons from the Early History of the Oxford English Dictionary," *Digital Studies/Le Champ Numérique* 6, no. 6 (2016), https://doi.org/10.16995/dscn.9.
84 This quotation is from the National Geographic Education website: https://education.nationalgeographic.org/resource/citizen-science/. An early influential book defining citizen science was Alan Irwin, *Citizen Science: A Study of People, Expertise and Sustainable Development* (London: Routledge, 1995). For a wide-ranging recent overview of key issues for citizen science, see Susanne Hecker, Muki Haklay, Anne Bowser, Zen Makuch, Johannes Vogel, and Aletta Bonn, eds., *Citizen Science: Innovation in Open Science, Society and Policy* (London: UCL Press, 2018).
85 Tim Berners-Lee, *Weaving the Web: The Original Design and Ultimate Destiny of the World Wide Web* (New York: HarperCollins, 2000), 123.

86 John Prpić, Araz Taeihagh, and James Melton, "The Fundamentals of Policy Crowdsourcing," *P & I: Policy & Internet* 7, no. 3 (2015): 340–61, https://doi.org/10.1002/poi3.102.

87 Arbuckle et al., "An Open Social Scholarship Path," 4. See, for example, Barbara Heinisch, Kristin Oswald, Maike Weißpflug, Sally Shuttleworth, and Geoffrey Belknap, "Citizen Humanities," in *The Science of Citizen Science*, ed. Katrin Vohland, Anne Land-Zandstra, Luigi Ceccaroni, Rob Lemmens, Josep Perelló, Marisa Ponti, Roeland Samson, and Katherin Wagenknecht (Cham, Switzerland: Springer, 2021), 97–118, https://doi.org/10.1007/978-3-030-58278-4_6. For discussion of crowdsourcing in the health field, to take the example of another discipline, see Kerri Wazny, "'Crowdsourcing' Ten Years In: A Review," *Journal of Global Health* 7, no. 2 (2017): art. 020601, https://doi.org/10.7189/jogh.07.020601.

88 Jeff Howe, "The Rise of Crowdsourcing," *Wired*, June 1, 2006, https://www.wired.com/2006/06/crowds/.

89 Melissa Terras, "Crowdsourcing in the Digital Humanities," in *A New Companion to Digital Humanities*, ed. Susan Schreibman, Ray Siemens, and John Unsworth (Chichester: Wiley & Sons, 2016), 4. Hedges and Dunn similarly refer to "the process of leveraging public participation in or contributions to projects or activities." Mark Hedges and Stuart Dunn, *Academic Crowdsourcing in the Humanities: Crowds, Communities and Co-Production* (Cambridge, MA: Chandos, 2017), 1.

90 See Daren C. Brabham, "Crowdsourcing as a Model for Problem Solving: An Introduction and Cases," *Convergence: The International Journal of Research into New Media Technologies* 14, no. 1 (2008): 75–90, https://doi.org/10.1177/1354856507084420.

91 https://www.mturk.com/.

92 https://www.microworkers.com/.

93 https://www.zooniverse.org/.

94 See Matthias Hirth, Jason Jacques, Peter Rodgers, Ognjen Scekic, and Michael Wybrow, "Crowdsourcing Technology to Support Academic Research," in *Evaluation in the Crowd: Crowdsourcing and Human-Centered Experiments*, ed. Daniel Archambault, Helen C. Purchase, and Tobias Hoßfeld (Cham, Switzerland: Springer, 2017), 70–95.

95 For example, see Matthew L. Smith and Ruhiya Kristine Seward, eds., *Making Open Development Inclusive: Lessons from IDRC Research* (Cambridge, MA: MIT Press, 2020). See also Christina Horvath and Juliet Carpenter, eds., *Co-Creation in Theory and Practice: Exploring Creativity in the Global North and South* (Bristol: Policy Press, 2020).

96 Hedges and Dunn, *Academic Crowdsourcing*, 1, 25, 33–8, 138.

97 In some humanities disciplines, public engagement is more established and expected. As Brennan notes, "Public history and humanities practices—in either digital or analog forms—place communities, or other public audiences, at their core." Sheila A. Brennan, "Public, First," in *Debates in the Digital Humanities 2016*, ed. Matthew K. Gold and Lauren F. Klein (Minneapolis: University of Minnesota Press, 2016), 384.

98 Victor de Boer, Michiel Hildebrand, Lora Aroyo, Pieter De Leenheer, Chris Dijkshoorn, Binyam Tesfa, and Guus Schreiber, "Nichesourcing: Harnessing the Power of Crowds of Experts," in *Knowledge Engineering and Knowledge Management*, EKAW 2012, Lecture Notes in Computer Science 7603 (Berlin: Springer, 2012), 16–20, https://doi.org/10.1007/978-3-642-33876-2_3.

99 https://www.wikipedia.org/. See Geoffrey Rockwell, "Crowdsourcing the Humanities: Social Research and Collaboration," in *Collaborative Research in the Digital Humanities*, ed. Marilyn Deegan and Willard McCarty (Farnham: Ashgate, 2012), 139.

100 Crowdsourcing has various definitions. See Enrique Estellés-Arolas and Fernando González-Ladrón-de-Guevara, "Towards an Integrated Crowdsourcing Definition," *Journal of Information Science* 38, no. 2 (2012): 189–200, https://doi.org/10.1177/0165551512437638. See also Daren C. Brabham, *Crowdsourcing* (Cambridge, MA: MIT Press, 2013), xix–xxii.

101 https://www.ucl.ac.uk/bentham-project/transcribe-bentham. See Tim Causer and Melissa Terras, "Crowdsourcing Bentham: Beyond the Traditional Boundaries of Academic History," *International Journal of Humanities and Arts Computing* 8, no. 1 (2014): 46–64, https://doi.org/10.3366/ijhac.2014.0119. For a foundational edited volume on cultural heritage crowdsourcing, see Mia Ridge, ed., *Crowdsourcing Our Cultural Heritage* (Farnham: Ashgate, 2014). For further discussion, see Chiara Bonacchi, Andrew Bevan, Adi Keinan-Schoonbaert, Daniel Pett, and Jennifer Wexler, "Participation in Heritage Crowdsourcing," *Museum Management and Curatorship* 34, no. 2 (2019): 166–82, https://doi.org/10.1080/09647775.2018.1559080.

102 https://crowdheritage.eu/.

103 https://www.europeana.eu/en.

104 https://trove.nla.gov.au/.

105 https://trove.nla.gov.au/frequently-asked-questions.

106 Concerns relate to the development of business-oriented aggregator platforms focused on large-scale approaches to repetitive micro-tasks. Hirth et al., "Crowdsourcing Technology." Participants are often only involved in a short-term way, especially if they have limited compensation or feedback. Nancy Ettlinger, "The Governance of Crowdsourcing: Rationalities of the New Exploitation," *Environment and Planning A: Economy and Space* 48, no. 11 (2016): 2162–80, https://doi.org/10.1177/0308518X16656182.

107 Trevar D. Riley-Reid, "The Hidden Cost of Digitization—Things to Consider," *Collection Building* 34, no. 3 (2015): 89–93, https://doi.org/10.1108/CB-01-2015-0001.

5 Reshaping How Universities Assess Research Impact

1 P. L. Gross and E. M. Gross, "College Libraries and Chemical Education," *Science* 66, no. 1713 (October 28, 1927): 385–9, https://doi.org/10.1126/science.66.1713.385. Cited in Lutz Bornmann and Hans-Dieter Daniel, "What Do Citation Counts Measure?: A Review of Studies on Citing Behavior," *Journal of Documentation* 64, no. 1 (2008): 45, https://doi.org/10.1108/00220410810844150.
2 Bornmann and Daniel, "What Do Citation Counts Measure?," 46. See also Lutz Bornmann, Robin Haunschild, and Rüdiger Mutz, "Growth Rates of Modern Science: A Latent Piecewise Growth Curve Approach to Model Publication Numbers from Established and New Literature Databases," *Humanities and Social Sciences Communications* 8 (2021): art. 224, https://doi.org/10.1057/s41599-021-00903-w.
3 Mike Thelwall and Maria M. Delgado, "Arts and Humanities Research Evaluation: No Metrics Please, Just Data," *Journal of Documentation* 71, no. 4 (2015): 817, https://doi.org/10.1108/JD-02-2015-0028.
4 The term was first used by Paul Otlet in his book *Traité de Documentation*. Quoted in Karen Blakeman, "Bibliometrics in a Digital Age: Help or Hindrance," *Science Progress* 101, no. 3 (2018): 293, https://doi.org/10.3184/003685018X15337564592469.
5 See Jorge E. Hirsch, "An Index to Quantify an Individual's Scientific Research Output," *Proceedings of the National Academy of Sciences* 102, no. 46 (2005): 16569–72, https://doi.org/10.1073/pnas.0507655102.
6 Bornmann and Daniel's review of studies on scientists' citing behavior outlines criticisms directed at citation analysis. See Bornmann and Daniel, "What Do Citation Counts Measure?"; Ian Rowlands, "What Are We Measuring?: Refocusing on Some Fundamentals in the Age of Desktop Bibliometrics," *FEMS Microbiology Letters* 365, no. 8 (2018): 2, see Table 1, fny059, https://doi.org/10.1093/femsle/fny059; Arlette Jappe, David Pithan, and Thomas Heinze, "Does Bibliometric Research Confer Legitimacy to Research Assessment Practice?: A Sociological Study of Reputational Control, 1972–2016," *PLOS ONE* 13, no. 6 (2018): e0199031, https://doi.org/10.1371/journal.pone.0199031.
7 Robert Adler, John Ewing, and Peter Taylor, "Citation Statistics: A Report from the International Mathematical Union (IMU) in Cooperation with the International Council of Industrial and Applied Mathematics (ICIAM) and the Institute of Mathematical Statistics (IMS)," *Statistical Science* 24, no. 1 (2009): 1–14, https://doi.org/10.1214/09-STS285.
8 Blaise Cronin, *The Citation Process: The Role and Significance of Citations in Scientific Communication* (London: Taylor Graham, 1984).

9. Yet studies show that in large collections of publications, these "biases may tend to even out," that is, "despite some citations being negative and despite the presence of some biasing factors." Thelwall and Delgado, "Arts and Humanities Research Evaluation," 818.

10. Rossana Morriello, "How Bibliometrics Is Affecting SSH," in *Proceedings of the ICTeSSH 2021 Conference,* July 20, 2021, https://doi.org/10.21428/7a458 13f.16c632d9.

11. Sabina Siebert, Laura M. Machesky, and Robert H. Insall, "Point of View: Overflow in Science and Its Implications for Trust," *eLife,* no. 4 (2015): e10825, https://doi.org/10.7554/eLife.10825.

12. Mark Murphy and Cristina Costa, "Digital Scholarship, Higher Education and the Future of the Public Intellectual," *Futures* 111 (2019): 208, https://doi.org/10.1016/j.futures.2018.04.011; Richard Watermeyer, "Public Intellectuals vs. New Public Management: The Defeat of Public Engagement in Higher Education," *Studies in Higher Education* 41, no. 12 (2016): 2271–85, https://doi.org/10.1080/03075079.2015.1034261.

13. Erin C. McKiernan, "Imagining the 'Open' University: Sharing Scholarship to Improve Research and Education," *PLOS Biology* 15, no. 10 (2017): e1002614, https://doi.org/10.1371/journal.pbio.1002614.

14. Jere Odell, Heather Coates, and Kristi Palmer, "Rewarding Open Access Scholarship in Promotion and Tenure: Driving Institutional Change," *College and Research Libraries News* 77, no. 7 (2016): 322–5, https://doi.org/10.5860/crln.77.7.9518.

15. Stefanie Haustein, "Grand Challenges in Altmetrics: Heterogeneity, Data Quality and Dependencies," *Scientometrics* 108, no. 1 (2016): 413–23, https://doi.org/10.1007/s11192-016-1910-9. For a North American perspective, see Wilhelm Peekhaus and Nicholas Proferes, "How Library and Information Science Faculty Perceive and Engage with Open Access," *Journal of Information Science* 41, no. 5 (2015): 640–61, https://doi.org/10.1177/0165551515587855; Odell, Coates, and Palmer, "Rewarding Open Access Scholarship."

16. Steffen Lemke, Maryam Mehrazar, Athanasios Mazarakis, and Isabella Peters, "'When You Use Social Media You Are Not Working': Barriers for the Use of Metrics in Social Sciences," *Frontiers in Research Metrics and Analytics* 3, no. 39 (2019), https://doi.org/10.3389/frma.2018.00039; Bhuva Narayan, Edward J. Luca, Belinda Tiffen, Ashley England, Mal Booth, and Henry Boateng, "Scholarly Communication Practices in Humanities and Social Sciences: A Study of Researchers' Attitudes and Awareness of Open Access," *Open Information Science* 2, no. 1 (2018): 168–80, https://doi.org/10.1515/opis-2018-0013.

17. Stephen Pinfield, "Making Open Access Work: The 'State-of-the-Art' in Providing Open Access to Scholarly Literature," *Online Information Review* 39, no. 5 (2015): 612–13, https://doi.org/10.1108/OIR-05-2015-0167.

18 Research Excellence Framework, *Research Excellence Framework 2014: Overview Report by Main Panel D and Sub-Panels 27 to 36*, January 2015, 17–18, https://www.ref.ac.uk/2014/media/ref/content/expanel/member/Main%20Panel%20D%20overview%20report.pdf; Jack Spaapen and Gunnar Sivertsen, "Assessing Societal Impact of SSH in an Engaging World: Focus on Productive Interaction, Creative Pathways and Enhanced Visibility of SSH Research," *Research Evaluation* 29, no. 1 (2020): 1–3, https://doi.org/10.1093/reseval/rvz035.
19 Research Excellence Framework, *Research Excellence Framework 2014*, 14.
20 Gunnar Sivertsen and Ingeborg Meijer, "Normal versus Extraordinary Societal Impact: How to Understand, Evaluate, and Improve Research Activities in Their Relations to Society?," *Research Evaluation* 29, no. 1 (2020): 66–70, https://doi.org/10.1093/reseval/rvz032; Elea Giménez Toledo, "Research Assessment in Humanities and Social Sciences in Review," *Revista Española de Documentación Científica* 41, no. 3 (2018): e208, https://doi.org/10.3989/redc.2018.3.1552.
21 "Crowdsourcing and Citizen Science Act of 2015," § S.2113 (United States Senate, 2015), https://www.congress.gov/bill/114th-congress/senate-bill/2113/text.
22 Nicolas Robinson-Garcia, Thed N. van Leeuwen, and Ismael Ràfols, "Using Altmetrics for Contextualised Mapping of Societal Impact: From Hits to Networks," *Science and Public Policy* 45, no. 6 (2018): 816, https://doi.org/10.1093/scipol/scy024.
23 McKiernan, "Imagining the 'Open' University."
24 Björn Hammarfelt and Sarah de Rijcke, "Accountability in Context: Effects of Research Evaluation Systems on Publication Practices, Disciplinary Norms, and Individual Working Routines in the Faculty of Arts at Uppsala University," *Research Evaluation* 24, no. 1 (2015): 75, https://doi.org/10.1093/reseval/rvu029; Jappe, Pithan, and Heinze, "Does Bibliometric Research Confer Legitimacy?"
25 San Francisco Declaration on Research Assessment, "San Francisco Declaration," 2013, https://sfdora.org/read/. For discussion, see Ross Cagan, "The San Francisco Declaration on Research Assessment," *Disease Models and Mechanisms* 6, no. 4 (July 2013): 869–70, https://doi.org/10.1242/dmm.012955.
26 Diana Hicks, Paul Wouters, Ludo Waltman, Sarah de Rijcke, and Ismael Rafols, "Leiden Manifesto for Research Metrics," 2015, http://www.leidenmanifesto.org/; Diana Hicks, Paul Wouters, Ludo Waltman, Sarah de Rijcke, and Ismael Rafols, "Bibliometrics: The Leiden Manifesto for Research Metrics," *Nature* 520, no. 7548 (2015): 429–31, https://doi.org/10.1038/520429a.
27 James Wilsdon, Liz Allen, Eleonora Belfiore, Philip Campbell, Stephen Curry, Steven Hill, Richard Jones, Roger Kain, Simon Kerridge, Mike Thelwall, Jane Tinkler, Ian Viney, Paul Wouters, Jude Hill, and Ben Johnson, *The Metric Tide: Report of the Independent Review of the Role of Metrics in Research Assessment and Management* (Higher Education Funding Council for England, 2015), https://doi.org/10.13140/RG.2.1.4929.1363.

28 Jason Priem and Bradley H. Hemminger, "Scientometrics 2.0: New Metrics of Scholarly Impact on the Social Web," *First Monday* 15, no. 7 (2010), https://doi.org/10.5210/fm.v15i7.2874; Jason Priem, "Altmetrics," in *Beyond Bibliometrics: Harnessing Multi-Dimensional Indicators of Performance*, ed. Blaise Cronin and Cassidy Sugimoto (Cambridge, MA: MIT Press, 2014), 263–88; Henk F. Moed and Gali Halevi, "Multidimensional Assessment of Scholarly Research Impact," *Journal of the Association for Information Science and Technology* 66, no. 10 (2015): 1988–2002, https://doi.org/10.1002/asi.23314.

29 Jason Priem, Dario Taraborelli, Paul Groth, and Cameron Neylon, "Altmetrics: A Manifesto," October 26, 2010, http://altmetrics.org/manifesto.

30 http://altmetrics.org/about/.

31 Heather Piwowar, "Altmetrics: Value All Research Products," *Nature* 493, no. 7431 (2013): 159, https://doi.org/10.1038/493159a; Paul Wouters, Zohreh Zahedi, and Rodrigo Costas, "Social Media Metrics for New Research Evaluation," in *Springer Handbook of Science and Technology Indicators*, ed. Wolfgang Glänzel, Henk F. Moed, Ulrich Baer, and Mike Thelwall (Cham, Switzerland: Springer, 2019), 687–713, https://doi.org/10.1007/978-3-030-02511-3_26.

32 Haustein, "Grand Challenges in Altmetrics," 416.

33 Christine Greenhow and Benjamin Gleason, "Social Scholarship: Reconsidering Scholarly Practices in the Age of Social Media," *British Journal of Educational Technology* 45, no. 3 (2014): 393–4, https://doi.org/10.1111/bjet.12150. See also the "Social Media in Academia" section of the follow-up article: Christine Greenhow, Benjamin Gleason, and K. Bret Staudt Willet, "Social Scholarship Revisited: Changing Scholarly Practices in the Age of Social Media," *British Journal of Educational Technology* 50, no. 3 (2019): 989–90, https://doi.org/10.1111/bjet.12772.

34 Ian Rowlands, David Nicholas, Bill Russell, Nicholas Canty, and Anthony Watkinson, "Social Media Use in the Research Workflow," *Learned Publishing* 24, no. 3 (2011): 183–95, https://doi.org/10.1087/20110306; Ali Al-Aufi and Crystal Fulton, "Impact of Social Networking Tools on Scholarly Communication: A Cross-Institutional Study," *Electronic Library* 33, no. 2 (2015): 224–41, https://doi.org/10.1108/EL-05-2013-0093. See also George Veletsianos, *Social Media in Academia: Networked Scholars* (New York: Routledge, 2016).

35 Carol Tenopir, Kenneth Levine, Suzie Allard, Lisa Christian, Rachel Volentine, Reid Boehm, Frances Nichols, David Nicholas, Hamid R. Jamali, Eti Herman, and Anthony Watkinson, "Trustworthiness and Authority of Scholarly Information in a Digital Age: Results of an International Questionnaire," *Journal of the Association for Information Science and Technology* 67, no. 10 (2016): 2344–61, https://doi.org/10.1002/asi.23598.

36 Murphy and Costa, "Digital Scholarship, Higher Education."

37 McKiernan, "Imagining the 'Open' University."
38 José Luis Ortega, "Disciplinary Differences of the Impact of Altmetric," *FEMS Microbiology Letters* 365, no. 7 (2018): fny049, https://doi.org/10.1093/femsle/fny 049; Adrián A. Díaz-Faes, Timothy D. Bowman, and Rodrigo Costas, "Towards a Second Generation of 'Social Media Metrics': Characterizing Twitter Communities of Attention around Science," *PLOS ONE* 14, no. 5 (2019): e0216408, https://doi.org/10.1371/journal.pone.0216408.
39 Lutz Bornmann, "Do Altmetrics Point to the Broader Impact of Research?: An Overview of Benefits and Disadvantages of Altmetrics," *Journal of Informetrics* 8, no. 4 (2014): 895–903, https://doi.org/10.1016/j.joi.2014.09.005; Cameron Neylon, Michelle Willmers, and Thomas King, "Rethinking Impact: Applying Altmetrics to Southern African Research," *Scholarly Communication in Africa: Rethinking Impact* (January 2014), https://open.uct.ac.za/bitstream/handle/11427/2285/SCAP_Neylon_RethinkingImpact_2014.pdf?sequence=1&isAllowed=y.
40 Bornmann, "Do Altmetrics Point to the Broader Impact of Research?"; McKiernan, "Imagining the 'Open' University"; Murphy and Costa, "Digital Scholarship, Higher Education"; Piwowar, "Altmetrics: Value All Research Products."
41 Robinson-Garcia, van Leeuwen, and Ràfols, "Using Altmetrics for Contextualised Mapping"; Pierre-Benoît Joly, Ariane Gaunand, Laurence Colinet, Philippe Larédo, Stéphane Lemarié, and Mireille Matt, "ASIRPA: A Comprehensive Theory-Based Approach to Assessing the Societal Impacts of a Research Organization," *Research Evaluation* 24, no. 4 (2015): 440–53, https://doi.org/10.1093/reseval/rvv015; Rodrigo Costas, Sarah de Rijcke, and Noortje Marres, "'Heterogeneous Couplings': Operationalizing Network Perspectives to Study Science–Society Interactions through Social Media Metrics," *Journal of the Association for Information Science and Technology* 72, no. 5 (2021): 595–610, https://doi.org/10.1002/asi.24427.
42 Cassidy R. Sugimoto, Sam Work, Vincent Larivière, and Stefanie Haustein, "Scholarly Use of Social Media and Altmetrics: A Review of the Literature," *Journal of the Association for Information Science and Technology* 68, no. 9 (2017): 2047, https://doi.org/10.1002/asi.23833.
43 Jennifer Lin and Martin Fenner, "Altmetrics in Evolution: Defining and Redefining the Ontology of Article-Level Metrics," *Information Standards Quarterly* 25, no. 2 (2013): 20–6, https://doi.org/10.3789/ISQV25NO2.2013.04. See also Haustein, "Grand Challenges in Altmetrics," 417. Haustein writes,

> Although many platforms now incorporate several functions, which aggravates classification, the following seven groups of social media platforms used for altmetrics are identified:
>
> (a) social networking (e.g., Facebook, ResearchGate)
> (b) social bookmarking and reference management (e.g., Mendeley, Zotero)

(c) social data sharing including sharing of datasets, software code, presentations, figures and videos, etc. (e.g., Figshare, Github)

(d) blogging (e.g., ResearchBlogging, Wordpress)

(e) microblogging (e.g., Twitter, Weibo)

(f) wikis (e.g., Wikipedia)

(g) social recommending, rating and reviewing (e.g., Reddit, F1000Prime)

The different purposes and functionalities of these platforms attract different audiences to perform various kinds of acts. (417)

44 https://plumanalytics.com/.
45 https://www.altmetric.com/. For discussion of various different services and their features, see Ortega, "Disciplinary Differences," 2.
46 Haustein, "Grand Challenges in Altmetrics," 418–19.
47 Robinson-Garcia, van Leeuwen, and Ràfols, "Using Altmetrics for Contextualised Mapping."
48 Joly et al., "ASIRPA," 440.
49 See Sugimoto et al., "Scholarly Use of Social Media and Altmetrics," 2047.
50 Haustein, "Grand Challenges in Altmetrics," 419.
51 Greenhow, Gleason, and Staudt Willet, "Social Scholarship Revisited"; Wilsdon et al., *The Metric Tide*; Stefanie Haustein, Timothy D. Bowman, and Rodrigo Costas, "Interpreting 'Altmetrics': Viewing Acts on Social Media through the Lens of Citation and Social Theories," in *Theories of Informetrics and Scholarly Communication*, ed. Cassidy R. Sugimoto (Berlin: De Gruyter Saur, 2016), 372–406, https://doi.org/10.1515/9783110308464-022.
52 Janet Finch, Simon Bell, Laura Bellingan, Robert Campbell, Peter Donnelly, Rita Gardner, Martin Hall, Steven Hall, Robert Kiley, and Wim van der Stelt, "Accessibility, Sustainability, Excellence: How to Expand Access to Research Publications—Executive Summary," *International Microbiology* 16, no. 2 (2013): 125–32, https://doi.org/10.2436/20.1501.01.187.
53 Martin Paul Eve, "Violins in the Subway: Scarcity Correlations, Evaluative Cultures, and Disciplinary Authority in the Digital Humanities," in *Digital Technology and the Practices of Humanities Research*, ed. Jennifer Edmond (Cambridge: Open Book, 2020), 114, https://doi.org/10.11647/OBP.0192. Eve gives the example of *PLOS ONE*, which as well as original research also sets out to publish negative results and replication studies.
54 Eike Mark Rinke and Alexander Wuttke, "Open Minds, Open Methods: Transparency and Inclusion in Pursuit of Better Scholarship," *PS: Political Science & Politics* 54, no. 2 (2021): 281, https://doi.org/10.1017/S1049096520001729; Marcel Knöchelmann, "Open Science in the Humanities, or: Open Humanities?," *Publications* 7, no. 4 (2019): art. 65, https://doi.org/10.3390/publications7040065.

55 Jonathan P. Tennant, Jonathan M. Dugan, Daniel Graziotin, Damien C. Jacques, François Waldner, Daniel Mietchen, Yehia Elkhatib, Lauren B. Collister, Christina K. Pikas, Tom Crick, Paola Masuzzo, Anthony Caravaggi, Devin R. Berg, Kyle E. Niemeyer, Tony Ross-Hellauer, Sara Mannheimer, Lillian Rigling, Daniel S. Katz, Bastian Greshake Tzovaras, Josmel Pacheko-Mendoza, Nazeefa Fatima, Marta Poblet, Marios Isaakidis, Dasapta Erwin Irawan, Sébastien Renaut, Christopher R. Madan, Lisa Matthias, Jesper Nørgaard Kjær, Daniel Paul O'Donnell, Cameron Neylon, Sarah Kearns, Manojkumar Selvaraju, and Julien Colomb, "A Multi-Disciplinary Perspective on Emergent and Future Innovations in Peer Review [Version 3; Peer Review: 2 Approved]," *F1000Research* 6 (2017): art. 1151, https://doi.org/10.12688/f1000research.12037.3.

56 Harry Crane and Ryan Martin, "In Peer Review We (Don't) Trust: How Peer Review's Filtering Poses a Systemic Risk to Science," *Researchers.One*, 2018, https://researchers.one/articles/18.09.00017v1; Cat Ferguson, Adam Marcus, and Ivan Oransky, "Publishing: The Peer-Review Scam," *Nature* 515, no. 7528 (2014): 480–2, https://doi.org/10.1038/515480a; Janine Huisman and Jeroen Smits, "Duration and Quality of the Peer Review Process: The Author's Perspective," *Scientometrics*, no. 113 (2017): 633–50, https://doi.org/10.1007/s11192-017-2310-5; Knöchelmann, "Open Science in the Humanities."

57 Birgit Schmidt, Tony Ross-Hellauer, Xenia van Edig, and Elizabeth C. Moylan, "Ten Considerations for Open Peer Review [Version 1; Peer Review: 2 Approved]," *F1000Research* 7 (2018): art. 969, https://doi.org/10.12688/f1000research.15334.1.

58 Maciej Maryl, Marta Błaszczyńska, Agnieszka Szulińska, and Paweł Rams, "The Case for an Inclusive Scholarly Communication Infrastructure for Social Sciences and Humanities [Version 1; Peer Review: 2 Approved]," *F1000Research* 9 (October 2020): 13, art. 1265, https://doi.org/10.12688/f1000research.26545.1.

59 Debates in the Digital Humanities (https://dhdebates.gc.cuny.edu/). See also Maryl et al., "Case for an Inclusive Scholarly Communication Infrastructure," 13–14. Open peer review is "moving more into the mainstream in a highly variable manner," and as such more research is called for to assess the most productive approaches. Jonathan P. Tennant and Tony Ross-Hellauer, "The Limitations to Our Understanding of Peer Review," *Research Integrity and Peer Review* 5, no. 6 (2020): 9, https://doi.org/10.1186/s41073-020-00092-1.

60 Pandelis Perakakis and Michael Taylor, "Academic Self-Publishing: A Not-So-Distant Future," *Prometheus: Critical Studies in Innovation* 31, no. 3 (2013): 257–63, https://doi.org/10.1080/08109028.2014.891712.

Conclusion: Pathways to Action

1. Globalization and competition have led to a "'reputation race' with geo-political implications." Ellen Hazelkorn, *Rankings and the Reshaping of Higher Education: The Battle for World-Class Excellence* (London: Palgrave Macmillan, 2015), 1, https://doi.org/10.1057/9781137446671.
2. In the early twenty-first century (2002), digital storage capacity for the first time surpassed that of total analog capacity, and the process has only accelerated. Martin Hilbert and Priscila López, "The World's Technological Capacity to Store, Communicate, and Compute Information," *Science* 332, no. 6025 (2011): 60–5, https://doi.org/10.1126/science.1200970.
3. The recent decision by Getty Images and other providers to ban AI-generated images in response to concerns over copyright violation is just one example of the potential challenges AI is bringing to existing regulations. See James Vincent, "Getty Images Bans AI-Generated Content over Fears of Legal Challenges," *The Verge*, September 21, 2022, https://www.theverge.com/2022/9/21/23364696/getty-images-ai-ban-generated-artwork-illustration-copyright. Writing this conclusion in mid-2023, the focus has now turned to ChatGPT and other AI platforms that may potentially be found to contravene plagiarism and copyright laws, and are a major cause for concern within education institutions.
4. Bhuva Narayan and Edward Luca, "Issues and Challenges in Researchers' Adoption of Open Access and Institutional Repositories: A Contextual Study of a University Repository," *Information Research* 22, no. 4 (2017), http://informationr.net/ir/22-4/rails/rails1608.html.
5. Jonathan P. Tennant, François Waldner, Damien C. Jacques, Paola Masuzzo, Lauren B. Collister, and Chris H. J. Hartgerink, "The Academic, Economic and Societal Impacts of Open Access: An Evidence-Based Review [Version 3; Peer Review: 4 Approved, 1 Approved with Reservations]," *F1000Research* 5 (2016): 3, art. 632, https://doi.org/10.12688/f1000research.8460.3.
6. Matthew L. Smith and Ruhiya Kristine Seward, eds., *Making Open Development Inclusive: Lessons from IDRC Research* (Cambridge, MA: MIT Press, 2020).
7. Jonathan Tennant, Jennifer Beamer, Jeroen Bosman, Björn Brembs, Neo Christopher Chung, Gail Clement, Tom Crick, Jonathan Dugan, Alastair Dunning, and David Eccles, "Foundations for Open Scholarship Strategy Development," *MetaArXiv*, January 30, 2019, https://doi.org/10.31222/osf.io/b4v8p.
8. Paul Longley Arthur, Lydia Hearn, Lucy Montgomery, Hugh Craig, Ray Siemens, and Alyssa Arbuckle, "Open Scholarship in Australia: A Review of Needs, Barriers and Opportunities," *Digital Scholarship in the Humanities* 36, no. 4 (2021): 795–812, https://doi.org/10.1093/llc/fqaa063.

Bibliography

Adler, Robert, John Ewing, and Peter Taylor. "Citation Statistics: A Report from the International Mathematical Union (IMU) in Cooperation with the International Council of Industrial and Applied Mathematics (ICIAM) and the Institute of Mathematical Statistics (IMS)." *Statistical Science* 24, no. 1 (2009): 1–14. https://doi.org/10.1214/09-STS285.

Al-Aufi, Ali, and Crystal Fulton. "Impact of Social Networking Tools on Scholarly Communication: A Cross-Institutional Study." *Electronic Library* 33, no. 2 (2015): 224–41. https://doi.org/10.1108/EL-05-2013-0093.

Albornoz, Denisse, Maggie Huang, Issra Martin, Maria Mateus, Aicha Touré, and Leslie Chan. "Framing Power: Tracing Key Discourses in Open Science Policies." In *ELPUB 2018*. Toronto, 2018. https://doi.org/10.4000/proceedings.elpub.2018.23.

Ali-Khan, Sarah E., Antoine Jean, and E. Richard Gold. "Identifying the Challenges in Implementing Open Science [Version 1; Peer Review: 2 Approved]." *MNI Open Research* 2, no. 5 (October 12, 2018). https://doi.org/10.12688/MNIOPENRES.12805.1.

Alperin, Juan Pablo. "The Public Impact of Latin America's Approach to Open Access." Stanford University, 2015. http://purl.stanford.edu/jr256tk1194.

Alperin, Juan Pablo, Carol Muñoz Nieves, Lesley Schimanski, Gustavo E. Fischman, Meredith T. Niles, and Erin C. McKiernan. "How Significant Are the Public Dimensions of Faculty Work in Review, Promotion, and Tenure Documents?" *Humanities Commons [Preprint]*, 2018. https://doi.org/10.17613/M6W950N35.

Alperin, Juan P., Carol Muñoz Nieves, Lesley A. Schimanski, Gustavo E. Fischman, Meredith T. Niles, and Erin C. McKiernan. "Meta-Research: How Significant Are the Public Dimensions of Faculty Work in Review, Promotion and Tenure Documents?" *eLife*, no. 8 (2019): e42254. https://doi.org/10.7554/eLife.42254.001.

Ancion, Zoé, Lidia Borrell-Damián, Pierre Mounier, Johan Rooryck, and Bregt Saenen. "Action Plan for Diamond Open Access." Zenodo, March 2022. https://doi.org/10.5281/zenodo.6282402.

Anderson, Rick. *Scholarly Communication: What Everyone Needs to Know*. Oxford: Oxford University Press, 2018.

Andrewes, William J. H., and Dava Sobel. *Longitude: The True Story of a Lone Genius Who Solved the Greatest Scientific Problem of His Time*. London: Fourth Estate, 1999.

Arbuckle, Alyssa. "Opportunities for Social Knowledge Creation in the Digital Humanities." In *Doing More Digital Humanities: Open Approaches to Creation,*

Growth, and Development, edited by Constance Crompton, Richard J. Lane, and Ray Siemens, 290–300. New York: Routledge, 2020.

Arbuckle, Alyssa, Ray Siemens, Jon Bath, Constance Crompton, Laura Estill, Tanja Niemann, Jon Saklofske, and Lynne Siemens. "An Open Social Scholarship Path for the Humanities." *Journal of Electronic Publishing* 25, no. 2 (2022). https://doi.org/10.3998/jep.1973.

Arthur, Paul Longley. "Tracing the Development of Digital Humanities in Australia." In *Digital Humanities and Scholarly Research Trends in the Asia-Pacific*, edited by Shun-han Rebekah Wong, Haipeng Li, and Min Chou, 1–18. Hershey, PA: IGI Global, 2019. https://doi.org/10.4018/978-1-5225-7195-7.ch001.

Arthur, Paul Longley, and Lydia Hearn. "Toward Open Research: A Narrative Review of the Challenges and Opportunities for Open Humanities." *Journal of Communication* 71, no. 5 (2021): 827–53. https://doi.org/10.1093/joc/jqab028.

Arthur, Paul Longley, Lydia Hearn, Lucy Montgomery, Hugh Craig, Ray Siemens, and Alyssa Arbuckle. "Open Scholarship in Australia: A Review of Needs, Barriers and Opportunities." *Digital Scholarship in the Humanities* 36, no. 4 (2021): 795–812. https://doi.org/10.1093/llc/fqaa063.

Baldwin, Melinda. "Peer Review." *Encyclopedia of the History of Science*, January 2020. https://doi.org/10.34758/srdejw27.

Banks, David. "Starting Science in the Vernacular: Notes on Some Early Issues of the *Philosophical Transactions* and the *Journal des Sçavans*, 1665–1700." *ASp: La Revue Du GERAS*, no. 55 (2009): 5–22. https://doi.org/10.4000/asp.213.

Barbour, Ginny. "The Future of Academic Publishing: Disruption, Opportunity and a New Ecosystem." *Medical Journal of Australia* 211, no. 4 (2019): 151–2. https://doi.org/10.5694/mja2.50265.

Barbour, Ginny, and Scott Nicholls. "Open Access: Should One Model Ever Fit All?" *Australian Quarterly* 90, no. 3 (2019): 3–9.

Barnet, Belinda. *Memory Machines: The Evolution of Hypertext*. London: Anthem Press, 2013.

Beaulieu, Marianne, Mylaine Breton, Astrid Brousselle, and Fiona Harris. "Conceptualizing 20 Years of Engaged Scholarship: A Scoping Review." *PLOS ONE* 13, no. 2 (2018): e0193201. https://doi.org/10.1371/journal.pone.0193201.

Benardou, Agiatis, Erik Champion, Costis Dallas, and Lorna M. Hughes, eds. *Cultural Heritage Infrastructures in Digital Humanities*. London: Routledge, 2018.

Benn, Jill, and Martin Borchert. "F.A.I.R. Is Fair for Research: Australian Initiatives to Improve Openness in the Scholarly Communications Environment." In *Proceedings of the IATUL Conferences*. Purdue University, Purdue e-Pubs, 2018.

Bennett, Scott. "Libraries and Learning: A History of Paradigm Change." *Portal: Libraries and the Academy* 9, no. 2 (2009): 181–97. https://doi.org/10.1353/pla.0.0049.

Berlin Declaration on Open Access to Knowledge in the Sciences and Humanities. "Berlin Declaration on Open Access to Knowledge in the Sciences and Humanities." October 22, 2003. https://openaccess.mpg.de/Berlin-Declaration.

Berners-Lee, Tim. *Weaving the Web: The Original Design and Ultimate Destiny of the World Wide Web*. New York: HarperCollins, 2000.

Bethesda Statement on Open Access Publishing. "Bethesda Statement on Open Access Publishing." June 20, 2003. https://dash.harvard.edu/bitstream/handle/1/4725199/Suber_bethesda.htm?sequence=3&isAllowed=y.

Bilder, G., J. Lin, and C. Neylon. "The Principles of Open Scholarly Infrastructure." 2020. https://doi.org/10.24343/C34W2H.

Blakeman, Karen. "Bibliometrics in a Digital Age: Help or Hindrance." *Science Progress* 101, no. 3 (2018): 293–310. https://doi.org/10.3184/003685018X15337564592469.

Boer, Victor de, Michiel Hildebrand, Lora Aroyo, Pieter De Leenheer, Chris Dijkshoorn, Binyam Tesfa, and Guus Schreiber. "Nichesourcing: Harnessing the Power of Crowds of Experts." In *Knowledge Engineering and Knowledge Management*, EKAW 2012, Lecture Notes in Computer Science 7603. Berlin: Springer, 2012. https://doi.org/10.1007/978-3-642-33876-2_3.

Bonacchi, Chiara, Andrew Bevan, Adi Keinan-Schoonbaert, Daniel Pett, and Jennifer Wexler. "Participation in Heritage Crowdsourcing." *Museum Management and Curatorship* 34, no. 2 (2019): 166–82. https://doi.org/10.1080/09647775.2018.1559080.

Borchert, Martin, Andrew Harrison, Andrew Heath, Belinda Tiffen, Janet Fletcher, Katrina Dewis, Maude Frances, Virginia Barbour, and Natasha Simons. *CAUL Fair, Affordable and Open Access to Knowledge Program: CAUL Review of Australian Repository Infrastructure*. Council of Australian University Librarians (CAUL), Australian Policy Online, March 15, 2019. https://apo.org.au/node/243791.

Borgerud, Charlotte, and Erik Borglund. "Open Research Data, An Archival Challenge?" *Archival Science*, no. 20 (2020): 279–302. https://doi.org/10.1007/s10502-020-09330-3.

Borgman, Christine L. *Big Data, Little Data, No Data: Scholarship in the Networked World*. Cambridge, MA: MIT Press, 2015.

Bornmann, Lutz. "Do Altmetrics Point to the Broader Impact of Research?: An Overview of Benefits and Disadvantages of Altmetrics." *Journal of Informetrics* 8, no. 4 (2014): 895–903. https://doi.org/10.1016/j.joi.2014.09.005.

Bornmann, Lutz, and Hans-Dieter Daniel. "What Do Citation Counts Measure?: A Review of Studies on Citing Behavior." *Journal of Documentation* 64, no. 1 (2008): 45–80. https://doi.org/10.1108/00220410810844150.

Bornmann, Lutz, Robin Haunschild, and Rüdiger Mutz. "Growth Rates of Modern Science: A Latent Piecewise Growth Curve Approach to Model Publication Numbers from Established and New Literature Databases." *Humanities and Social Sciences Communications* 8 (2021): art. 224. https://doi.org/10.1057/s41599-021-00903-w.

Borrego, Ángel, Lluís Anglada, and Ernest Abadal. "Transformative Agreements: Do They Pave the Way to Open Access?" *Learned Publishing* 34, no. 2 (2021): 216–32. https://doi.org/10.1002/leap.1347.

Boyer, Ernest L. "The Scholarship of Engagement." *Bulletin of the American Academy of Arts and Sciences* 49, no. 7 (1996): 18–33. https://doi.org/10.2307/3824459.

Brabham, Daren C. *Crowdsourcing*. Cambridge, MA: MIT Press, 2013.

Brabham, Daren C. "Crowdsourcing as a Model for Problem Solving: An Introduction and Cases." *Convergence: The International Journal of Research into New Media Technologies* 14, no. 1 (2008): 75–90. https://doi.org/10.1177/1354856507084420.

Brennan, Sheila A. "Public, First." In *Debates in the Digital Humanities 2016*, edited by Matthew K. Gold and Lauren F. Klein, 384–9. Minneapolis: University of Minnesota Press, 2016.

Budapest Open Access Initiative. "Budapest Open Access Initiative." February 14, 2002. https://www.budapestopenaccessinitiative.org/read.

Budapest Open Access Initiative. "Budapest Open Access Initiative: 20th Anniversary Recommendations." March 15, 2022. https://www.budapestopenaccessinitiative.org/boai20/.

Budapest Open Access Initiative. "Prologue: The Budapest Open Access Initiative after 10 Years." September 12, 2012. https://www.budapestopenaccessinitiative.org/boai10/.

Buddenbohm, Stefan, Nathanael Cretin, Elly Dijk, Bertrand Gaiffe, Maaike de Jong, Jean-Luc Minel, and Nathalie Le Tellier-Becquart. "State of the Art Report on Open Access Publishing of Research Data in the Humanities." DARIAH, 2016. https://halshs.archives-ouvertes.fr/halshs-01357208v3.

Burgelman, Jean-Claude, Corina Pascu, Katarzyna Szkuta, Rene Von Schomberg, Athanasios Karalopoulos, Konstantinos Repanas, and Michel Schouppe. "Open Science, Open Data, and Open Scholarship: European Policies to Make Science Fit for the Twenty-First Century." *Frontiers in Big Data* 2 (2019): 43. https://doi.org/10.3389/fdata.2019.00043.

Burke, Kelly. "Trove: National Library of Australia's Digital Archives Thrown $33m Lifeline by Federal Government." *Guardian*, April 3, 2023, Australia edition. https://www.theguardian.com/books/2023/apr/03/trove-national-library-of-australias-digital-archives-thrown-33m-lifeline-by-federal-government.

Bush, Vannevar. "As We May Think." *The Atlantic*, July 1945.

Bush, Vannevar. *Science: The Endless Frontier*. Washington, DC: US Government Printing Office, 1945. https://www.nsf.gov/od/lpa/nsf50/vbush1945.htm.

Cagan, Ross. "The San Francisco Declaration on Research Assessment." *Disease Models and Mechanisms* 6, no. 4 (July 2013): 869–70. https://doi.org/10.1242/dmm.012955.

The Cape Town Open Education Declaration. "The Cape Town Open Education Declaration: Unlocking the Promise of Open Educational Resources," September 2007. https://www.capetowndeclaration.org/.

Carroll, Stephanie Russo, Ibrahim Garba, Oscar L. Figueroa-Rodríguez, Jarita Holbrook, Raymond Lovett, Simeon Materechera, Mark Parsons, Kay Raseroka, Desi Rodriguez-Lonebear, Robyn Rowe, Rodrigo Sara, Jennifer D. Walker, Jane Anderson, and Maui Hudson. "The CARE Principles for Indigenous Data

Governance." *Data Science Journal* 19, no. 1 (2020): art. 43. https://doi.org/10.5334/dsj-2020-043.

Causer, Tim, and Melissa Terras. "Crowdsourcing Bentham: Beyond the Traditional Boundaries of Academic History." *International Journal of Humanities and Arts Computing* 8, no. 1 (2014): 46–64. https://doi.org/10.3366/ijhac.2014.0119.

Chan, Leslie, Barbara Kirsop, and Subbiah Arunachalam. "Towards Open and Equitable Access to Research and Knowledge for Development." *PLOS Medicine* 8, no. 3 (2011): e1001016. https://doi.org/10.1371/journal.pmed.1001016.

Chase, Darren, and Dana Haugh, eds. *Open Praxis, Open Access: Digital Scholarship in Action*. Chicago: ALA Editions, 2020.

Chubin, Daryl E. "Open Science and Closed Science: Tradeoffs in a Democracy." *Science, Technology, & Human Values* 10, no. 2 (1985): 73–81.

Clemons, Jessica. "Open Science and Open Data: What Can We Learn from the Open Access Movement?" In *Open Praxis, Open Access: Digital Scholarship in Action*, edited by Darren Chase and Dana Haugh, 211–24. Chicago: ALA Editions, 2020.

CODATA (Committee on Data of the International Science Council), Simon Hodson, Barend Mons, Paul Uhlir, and Lili Zhang. "The Beijing Declaration on Research Data." Zenodo, November 25, 2019. https://doi.org/10.5281/zenodo.3552329.

Collins, Sandra, Natalie Harrower, Dag Trygve Truslew Haug, Beat Immenhauser, Gerhard Lauer, Tito Orlandi, Laurent Romary, and Eveline Wandl-Vogt. *Going Digital: Creating Change in the Humanities*. Berlin: ALLEA All European Academies, 2015. https://www.allea.org/wp-content/uploads/2015/07/Going-Digital_digital-version.pdf.

Confederation of Open Access Repositories. "The Case for Interoperability for Open Access Repositories: Working Group 2—Repository Interoperability." July 8, 2011.

Copyright, Designs and Patents Act 1988 (c. 48), United Kingdom, 1988. https://www.legislation.gov.uk/ukpga/1988/48/enacted.

Costas, Rodrigo, Sarah de Rijcke, and Noortje Marres. "'Heterogeneous Couplings': Operationalizing Network Perspectives to Study Science–Society Interactions through Social Media Metrics." *Journal of the Association for Information Science and Technology* 72, no. 5 (2021): 595–610. https://doi.org/10.1002/asi.24427.

Council of Australian University Librarians. "CAUL Statement on Open Scholarship 2019." https://www.caul.edu.au/programs-projects/advancing-open-scholarship-fair/statement-open-scholarship.

Cox, Brian. "The Pergamon Phenomenon 1951–1991: Robert Maxwell and Scientific Publishing." *Learned Publishing* 15, no. 4 (2002): 273–8. https://doi.org/10.1087/095315102760319233.

Crane, Harry, and Ryan Martin. "In Peer Review We (Don't) Trust: How Peer Review's Filtering Poses a Systemic Risk to Science." *Researchers.One*, 2018. https://researchers.one/articles/18.09.00017v1.

Cronin, Blaise. *The Citation Process: The Role and Significance of Citations in Scientific Communication*. London: Taylor Graham, 1984.

Crow, Michael M., and William B. Dabars. *The Fifth Wave: The Evolution of American Higher Education*. Baltimore: Johns Hopkins University Press, 2020.

Crowdsourcing and Citizen Science Act of 2015, § S.2113. United States Senate, 2015. https://www.congress.gov/bill/114th-congress/senate-bill/2113/text.

Dallas, Costis, Nephelie Chatzidaiakou, Agiatis Benardou, Michael Bender, Aurélien Berra, Claire Clivaz, John Cunningham, Meredith Dabek, Patricia Garrido, Elena Gonzalez-Blanco, Jurij Hadalin, Lorna Hughes, Beat Immenhauser, Anne Joly, Ingrida Kelpšienė, Michał Kozak, Koraljka Kuzman, Marko Lukin, Irena Marinski, Maciej Maryl, Robert Owain, Eliza Papaki, Gerlinde Schneider, Walter Scholger, Susan Schreibman, Zoe Schubert, Toma Tasovac, Manfred Thaller, Piotr Wciślik, Marcin Werla, and Tvrtko Zebec. "European Survey on Scholarly Practices and Digital Needs in the Arts and Humanities: Survey Highlights." In *Digital Methods and Practices Observatory Working Group (DiMPO), DARIAH-EU European Research Infrastructure Consortium*. DARIAH-EU, October 2016.

Daniels, Jessie, and Polly Thistlethwaite. *Being a Scholar in the Digital Era: Transforming Scholarly Practice for the Public Good*. Bristol: Policy Press, 2016.

Deazley, Ronan. *Rethinking Copyright: History, Theory, Language*. Cheltenham: Edward Elgar, 2006.

Deegan, Marilyn, and Kathryn Sutherland. *Transferred Illusions: Digital Technology and the Forms of Print*. Farnham: Ashgate, 2009.

Díaz-Faes, Adrián A., Timothy D. Bowman, and Rodrigo Costas. "Towards a Second Generation of 'Social Media Metrics': Characterizing Twitter Communities of Attention around Science." *PLOS ONE* 14, no. 5 (2019): e0216408. https://doi.org/10.1371/journal.pone.0216408.

Dienlin, Tobias, Niklas Johannes, Nicholas David Bowman, Philipp K. Masur, Sven Engesser, Anna Sophie Kümpel, Josephine Lukito, Lindsey M. Bier, Renwen Zhang, Benjamin K. Johnson, Richard Huskey, Frank M. Schneider, Johannes Breuer, Douglas A. Parry, Ivar Vermeulen, Jacob T. Fisher, Jaime Banks, René Weber, David A. Ellis, Tim Smits, James D. Ivory, Sabine Trepte, Bree McEwan, Eike Mark Rinke, German Neubaum, Stephan Winter, Christopher J. Carpenter, Nicole Krämer, Sonja Utz, Julian Unkel, Xiaohui Wang, Brittany I. Davidson, Nuri Kim, Andrea Stevenson Won, Emese Domahidi, Neil A. Lewis, and Claes de Vreese. "An Agenda for Open Science in Communication." *Journal of Communication* 71, no. 1 (2020): 1–26. https://doi.org/10.1093/joc/jqz052.

Dodds, Francis. "The Changing Copyright Landscape in Academic Publishing." *Learned Publishing* 31, no. 3 (2018): 270–5. https://doi.org/10.1002/leap.1157.

Dutton, William H. "Reconfiguring Access in Research: Information, Expertise, and Experience." In *World Wide Research: Reshaping the Sciences and Humanities*, edited by William H. Dutton and Paul W. Jeffreys, 21–39. Cambridge, MA: MIT Press, 2010.

Eamon, William. "From the Secrets of Nature to Public Knowledge: The Origins of the Concept of Openness in Science." *Minerva* 23, no. 3 (1985): 321–47.

Eger, Thomas, and Marc Scheufen. *The Economics of Open Access: On the Future of Academic Publishing*. Cheltenham: Edward Elgar, 2018.

"Electronic Freedom of Information Act Amendments of 1996 Public Law 1-4-238-Oct. 2, 1996" (1996). https://www.congress.gov/bill/104th-congress/house-bill/3802/text.

Estellés-Arolas, Enrique, and Fernando González-Ladrón-de-Guevara. "Towards an Integrated Crowdsourcing Definition." *Journal of Information Science* 38, no. 2 (2012): 189–200. https://doi.org/10.1177/0165551512437638.

Ettlinger, Nancy. "The Governance of Crowdsourcing: Rationalities of the New Exploitation." *Environment and Planning A: Economy and Space* 48, no. 11 (2016): 2162–80. https://doi.org/10.1177/0308518X16656182.

European Commission, Directorate-General for Communications Networks, Content and Technology. "European Cloud Initiative: Building a Competitive Data and Knowledge Economy in Europe—Document 52016DC0178." Brussels: European Commission, April 19, 2016. https://eur-lex.europa.eu/legal-content/EN/TXT/?qid=1555074889405&uri=CELEX:52016DC0178.

European Commission, Directorate-General for Research and Innovation. *Future of Scholarly Publishing and Scholarly Communication: Report of the Expert Group to the European Commission*. Brussels: European Commission, January 2019. https://data.europa.eu/doi/10.2777/836532.

European Science Foundation. "Plan S: Making Full and Immediate Open Access a Reality." Brussels: European Commission and the European Research Council, 2018. https://www.coalition-s.org/.

Eve, Martin Paul, ed. *Open Access and the Humanities: Contexts, Controversies and the Future*. Cambridge: Cambridge University Press, 2014.

Eve, Martin Paul. "Open Access Publishing Models and How OA Can Work in the Humanities." *Bulletin of the Association for Information Science and Technology* 43, no. 5 (2017): 16–20. https://doi.org/10.1002/bul2.2017.1720430505.

Eve, Martin Paul. "Violins in the Subway: Scarcity Correlations, Evaluative Cultures, and Disciplinary Authority in the Digital Humanities." In *Digital Technology and the Practices of Humanities Research*, edited by Jennifer Edmond, 105–22. Cambridge: Open Book, 2020. https://doi.org/10.11647/OBP.0192.

Fecher, Benedikt, and Sascha Friesike. "Open Science: One Term, Five Schools of Thought." In *Opening Science: The Evolving Guide on How the Internet Is Changing Research, Collaboration and Scholarly Publishing*, edited by Sönke Bartling and Sascha Friesike, 17–47. Cham, Switzerland: Springer, 2014. https://doi.org/10.1007/978-3-319-00026-8_2.

Ferguson, Cat, Adam Marcus, and Ivan Oransky. "Publishing: The Peer-Review Scam." *Nature* 515, no. 7528 (2014): 480–2. https://doi.org/10.1038/515480a.

Finch, Janet, Simon Bell, Laura Bellingan, Robert Campbell, Peter Donnelly, Rita Gardner, Martin Hall, Steven Hall, Robert Kiley, and Wim van der Stelt.

"Accessibility, Sustainability, Excellence: How to Expand Access to Research Publications—Executive Summary." *International Microbiology* 16, no. 2 (2013): 125–32. https://doi.org/10.2436/20.1501.01.187.

Fitzpatrick, Kathleen. *Planned Obsolescence: Publishing, Technology, and the Future of the Academy*. New York: New York University Press, 2011.

Fölster, Max Jakob. "Libraries and Archives in the Former Han Dynasty (206 BCE–9 CE): Arguing for a Distinction." In *Manuscripts and Archives: Comparative Views on Record-Keeping*, edited by Alessandro Bausi, Christian Brockmann, Michael Friedrich, and Sabine Kienitz, 201–30. Berlin: De Gruyter, 2018. https://doi.org/10.1515/9783110541397.

Foucault, Michel. *Power/Knowledge: Selected Interviews and Other Writings, 1972–1977 by Michel Foucault*. Edited by Colin Gordon. Translated by Colin Gordon, Leo Marshall, John Mepham, and Kate Soper. New York: Pantheon Books, 1980.

"The Freedom of Information Act. 5 U.S.C. § 552 as Amended by Public Law No. 110-175, 121 Stat. 2524" (2007). http://www.justice.gov/sites/default/files/oip/legacy/2014/07/23/amended-foia-redlined.pdf.

Fry, Sandra. "Five Open Access Tips for 21st-Century Researchers: Tip #1." *QUT Library* (blog), October 21, 2019. https://blogs.qut.edu.au/library/2019/10/21/five-open-access-tips-for-21st-century-researchers-tip-1/.

Fyfe, Aileen, Kelly Coate, Stephen Curry, Stuart Lawson, Noah Moxham, and Camilla Mørk Røstvik. "Untangling Academic Publishing: A History of the Relationship between Commercial Interests, Academic Prestige and the Circulation of Research." Zenodo, May 2017. https://doi.org/10.5281/zenodo.546100.

Gabler, Hans Walter. "Textual Criticism." In *The Johns Hopkins Guide to Literary Theory and Criticism*, 2nd ed., edited by Imre Szeman, Martin Kreiswirth, and Michael Groden, 901–8. Baltimore: Johns Hopkins University Press, 2005.

Gillespie, Tarleton. *Wired Shut: Copyright and the Shape of Digital Culture*. Cambridge, MA: MIT Press, 2007.

Greenhow, Christine, and Benjamin Gleason. "Social Scholarship: Reconsidering Scholarly Practices in the Age of Social Media." *British Journal of Educational Technology* 45, no. 3 (2014): 392–402. https://doi.org/10.1111/bjet.12150.

Greenhow, Christine, Benjamin Gleason, and K. Bret Staudt Willet. "Social Scholarship Revisited: Changing Scholarly Practices in the Age of Social Media." *British Journal of Educational Technology* 50, no. 3 (2019): 987–1004. https://doi.org/10.1111/bjet.12772.

Gross, Julia, and John Charles Ryan. "Landscapes of Research: Perceptions of Open Access (OA) Publishing in the Arts and Humanities." *Publications* 3, no. 2 (2015): 65–88. https://doi.org/10.3390/publications3020065.

Gross, P. L., and E. M. Gross. "College Libraries and Chemical Education." *Science* 66, no. 1713 (October 28, 1927): 385–9. https://doi.org/10.1126/science.66.1713.385.

G20 Summit. "G20 Leaders' Communique Hangzhou Summit." European Union, September 5, 2016. https://ec.europa.eu/commission/presscorner/detail/en/STATEMENT_16_2967.

Guédon, Jean-Claude. "Open Access: Toward the Internet of the Mind." Budapest Open Access Initiative, 2017. https://www.budapestopenaccessinitiative.org/boai15/open-access-toward-the-internet-of-the-mind/.

Hammarfelt, Björn. "Four Claims on Research Assessment and Metric Use in the Humanities." *Bulletin of the Association for Information Science and Technology* 43, no. 5 (2017): 33–8. https://doi.org/10.1002/bul2.2017.1720430508.

Hammarfelt, Björn, and Gaby Haddow. "Conflicting Measures and Values: How Humanities Scholars in Australia and Sweden Use and React to Bibliometric Indicators." *Journal of the Association for Information Science and Technology* 69, no. 7 (2018): 924–35. https://doi.org/10.1002/asi.24043.

Hammarfelt, Björn, and Sarah de Rijcke. "Accountability in Context: Effects of Research Evaluation Systems on Publication Practices, Disciplinary Norms, and Individual Working Routines in the Faculty of Arts at Uppsala University." *Research Evaluation* 24, no. 1 (2015): 63–77. https://doi.org/10.1093/reseval/rvu029.

Hampson, Glenn, Mel DeSart, Jason Steinhauer, Elizabeth A. Gadd, Lisa Janicke Hinchliffe, Micah Vandegrift, Chris Erdmann, and Rob Johnson. "OSI Policy Perspective 3: Open Science Roadmap Recommendations to UNESCO." *OSI Policy Perspectives, Open Scholarship Initiative*, June 2020. https://doi.org/10.13021/osi2020.2735.

Haustein, Stefanie. "Grand Challenges in Altmetrics: Heterogeneity, Data Quality and Dependencies." *Scientometrics* 108, no. 1 (2016): 413–23. https://doi.org/10.1007/s11192-016-1910-9.

Haustein, Stefanie, Timothy D. Bowman, and Rodrigo Costas. "Interpreting 'Altmetrics': Viewing Acts on Social Media through the Lens of Citation and Social Theories." In *Theories of Informetrics and Scholarly Communication*, edited by Cassidy R. Sugimoto, 372–406. Berlin: De Gruyter Saur, 2016. https://doi.org/10.1515/9783110308464-022.

Hazelkorn, Ellen. *Rankings and the Reshaping of Higher Education: The Battle for World-Class Excellence*. London: Palgrave Macmillan, 2015. https://doi.org/10.1057/9781137446671.

Hecker, Susanne, Muki Haklay, Anne Bowser, Zen Makuch, Johannes Vogel, and Aletta Bonn, eds. *Citizen Science: Innovation in Open Science, Society and Policy*. London: UCL Press, 2018.

Hedges, Mark, and Stuart Dunn. *Academic Crowdsourcing in the Humanities: Crowds, Communities and Co-Production*. Cambridge, MA: Chandos, 2017.

Heinisch, Barbara, Kristin Oswald, Maike Weißpflug, Sally Shuttleworth, and Geoffrey Belknap. "Citizen Humanities." In *The Science of Citizen Science*, edited by Katrin Vohland, Anne Land-Zandstra, Luigi Ceccaroni, Rob Lemmens, Josep Perelló,

Marisa Ponti, Roeland Samson, and Katherin Wagenknecht, 97–118. Cham, Switzerland: Springer, 2021. https://doi.org/10.1007/978-3-030-58278-4_6.

Hess, Charlotte, and Elinor Ostrom, eds. *Understanding Knowledge as a Commons: From Theory to Practice*. Cambridge, MA: MIT Press, 2007.

Hetland, Per, Palmyre Pierroux, and Line Esborg, eds. *A History of Participation in Museums and Archives: Traversing Citizen Science and Citizen Humanities*. London: Routledge, 2020.

Hicks, Diana, Paul Wouters, Ludo Waltman, Sarah de Rijcke, and Ismael Rafols. "Bibliometrics: The Leiden Manifesto for Research Metrics." *Nature* 520, no. 7548 (2015): 429–31. https://doi.org/10.1038/520429a.

Hicks, Diana, Paul Wouters, Ludo Waltman, Sarah de Rijcke, and Ismael Rafols. "Leiden Manifesto for Research Metrics." 2015. http://www.leidenmanifesto.org/.

Hilbert, Martin, and Priscila López. "The World's Technological Capacity to Store, Communicate, and Compute Information." *Science* 332, no. 6025 (2011): 60–5. https://doi.org/10.1126/science.1200970.

Hirsch, Jorge E. "An Index to Quantify an Individual's Scientific Research Output." *Proceedings of the National Academy of Sciences* 102, no. 46 (2005): 16569–72. https://doi.org/10.1073/pnas.0507655102.

Hirth, Matthias, Jason Jacques, Peter Rodgers, Ognjen Scekic, and Michael Wybrow. "Crowdsourcing Technology to Support Academic Research." In *Evaluation in the Crowd: Crowdsourcing and Human-Centered Experiments*, edited by Daniel Archambault, Helen C. Purchase, and Tobias Hoßfeld, 70–95. Cham, Switzerland: Springer, 2017.

Holzman, Alex. "US Open Access Publishing for the Humanities and Social Sciences." *European Political Science* 15, no. 2 (2016): 177–82. https://doi.org/10.1057/eps.2015.85.

Horvath, Christina, and Juliet Carpenter, eds. *Co-Creation in Theory and Practice: Exploring Creativity in the Global North and South*. Bristol: Policy Press, 2020.

Howe, Jeff. "The Rise of Crowdsourcing." *Wired*, June 1, 2006. https://www.wired.com/2006/06/crowds/.

Huisman, Janine, and Jeroen Smits. "Duration and Quality of the Peer Review Process: The Author's Perspective." *Scientometrics*, no. 113 (2017): 633–50. https://doi.org/10.1007/s11192-017-2310-5.

Irwin, Alan. *Citizen Science: A Study of People, Expertise and Sustainable Development*. London: Routledge, 1995.

Jappe, Arlette, David Pithan, and Thomas Heinze. "Does Bibliometric Research Confer Legitimacy to Research Assessment Practice?: A Sociological Study of Reputational Control, 1972–2016." *PLOS ONE* 13, no. 6 (2018): e0199031. https://doi.org/10.1371/journal.pone.0199031.

Jhangiani, Rajiv S., and Robert Biswas-Diener, eds. *Open: The Philosophy and Practices That Are Revolutionizing Education and Science*. London: Ubiquity Press, 2017.

Johnson, Eric. "On a Definition of 'Open Humanities.'" *Eric D. M. Johnson* (blog), April 2, 2012. https://www.ericdmjohnson.com/2012/04/02/on-a-definition-of-open-humanities/.

Joly, Pierre-Benoît, Ariane Gaunand, Laurence Colinet, Philippe Larédo, Stéphane Lemarié, and Mireille Matt. "ASIRPA: A Comprehensive Theory-Based Approach to Assessing the Societal Impacts of a Research Organization." *Research Evaluation* 24, no. 4 (2015): 440–53. https://doi.org/10.1093/reseval/rvv015.

Kingsley, Danny. "Build It and They Will Come?: Support for Open Access in Australia." *Scholarly Research Communication* 4, no. 1 (2013): art. 010137. https://doi.org/10.22230/src.2013v4n1a39.

Knöchelmann, Marcel. "Open Science in the Humanities, or: Open Humanities?" *Publications* 7, no. 4 (2019): art. 65. https://doi.org/10.3390/publications7040065.

Koltay, Tibor. "Quality of Open Research Data: Values, Convergences and Governance." *Information* 11, no. 4 (2020): 175. https://doi.org/10.3390/info11040175.

Koutras, Nikos. *Building Equitable Access to Knowledge through Open Access Repositories*. Hershey, PA: IGI Global, 2019.

Kraker, Peter, Daniel Dörler, Andreas Ferus, Robert Gutounig, Florian Heigl, Christian Kaier, Katharina Rieck, Elena Šimukovič, and Michela Vignoli. "Vienna Principles: A Vision for Scholarly Communication." 2016. https://viennaprinciples.org/.

Kronick, David A. *A History of Scientific and Technical Periodicals: The Origins and Development of the Scientific and Technological Press, 1665–1790*. New York: Scarecrow Press, 1962.

Lämmerhirt, Danny, Ana Brandusescu, Natalia Domagala, and Patrick Enaholo, eds. *Situating Open Data: Global Trends in Local Contexts*. Cape Town: African Minds, 2020.

Laporte, Steven. "Preprint for the Humanities: Fiction or a Real Possibility?" *Studia Historiae Scientiarum* 16 (2017): 367–78. https://doi.org/10.4467/2543702X SHS.17.014.7715.

Larivière, Vincent, Stefanie Haustein, and Philippe Mongeon. "The Oligopoly of Academic Publishers in the Digital Era." *PLOS ONE* 10, no. 6 (2015): e0127502. https://doi.org/10.1371/journal.pone.0127502.

Lazerson, Marvin. "The Disappointments of Success: Higher Education after World War II." *Annals of the American Academy of Political and Social Science* 559 (The Changing Educational Quality of the Workforce) (September 1998): 64–76.

Lemke, Steffen, Maryam Mehrazar, Athanasios Mazarakis, and Isabella Peters. "'When You Use Social Media You Are Not Working': Barriers for the Use of Metrics in Social Sciences." *Frontiers in Research Metrics and Analytics* 3, no. 39 (2019). https://doi.org/10.3389/frma.2018.00039.

Lessig, Lawrence. *Free Culture: How Big Media Uses Technology and the Law to Lock Down Culture and Control Creativity*. New York: Penguin, 2004.

Lewi, Hannah, Wally Smith, Dirk vom Lehn, and Steven Cooke, eds. *The Routledge International Handbook of New Digital Practices in Galleries, Libraries, Archives, Museums and Heritage Sites*. Abingdon: Routledge, 2020.

Lewis, Vivian, Lisa Spiro, Xuemao Wang, and Jon E. Cawthorne. *Building Expertise to Support Digital Scholarship: A Global Perspective*. Washington, DC: Council on Library and Information Resources, 2015. https://www.clir.org/pubs/reports/pub168/.

Lin, Jennifer, and Martin Fenner. "Altmetrics in Evolution: Defining and Redefining the Ontology of Article-Level Metrics." *Information Standards Quarterly* 25, no. 2 (2013): 20–6. https://doi.org/10.3789/ISQV25NO2.2013.04.

Liu, Yin. "Appeal to the Public: Lessons from the Early History of the Oxford English Dictionary." *Digital Studies/Le Champ Numérique* 6, no. 6 (2016). https://doi.org/10.16995/dscn.9.

Lorimer, Rowland. "Libraries, Scholars and Publishers in Digital Journal and Monograph Publishing." *Scholarly and Research Communication* 4, no. 1 (2013): art. 010136. https://doi.org/10.22230/src.2013v4n1a43.

Lund, Arwid, and Mariano Zukerfeld. *Corporate Capitalism's Use of Openness: Profit for Free?* Cham, Switzerland: Palgrave Macmillan, 2020.

Lynch, Clifford. "Guest Editorial: Updating the Agenda for Academic Libraries and Scholarly Communications." *College and Research Libraries* 78, no. 2 (2017): 126–30. https://doi.org/10.5860/crl.78.2.126.

Márquez, Melissa C., and Ana Maria Porras. "Science Communication in Multiple Languages Is Critical to Its Effectiveness." *Frontiers in Communication* 5 (2020). https://doi.org/10.3389/fcomm.2020.00031.

Martin, Victoria. "The Concept of Openness in Scholarship." In *Open Praxis, Open Access: Digital Scholarship in Action*, edited by Darren Chase and Dana Haugh, 3–19. Chicago: ALA Editions, 2020.

Maryl, Maciej, Marta Błaszczyńska, Agnieszka Szulińska, and Paweł Rams. "The Case for an Inclusive Scholarly Communication Infrastructure for Social Sciences and Humanities [Version 1; Peer Review: 2 Approved]." *F1000Research* 9 (October 2020): art. 1265. https://doi.org/10.12688/f1000research.26545.1.

Maryl, Maciej, Tito Orlandi, Bernard Rentier, and Eveline Wandl-Vogt. "Sustainable and FAIR Data Sharing in the Humanities." *Recommendations of the ALLEA Working Group E-Humanities*. Berlin: ALLEA All European Academies, February 2020. https://doi.org/10.7486/DRI.tq582c863.

Mayo, Marjorie. *Community-Based Learning and Social Movements*. Bristol: Policy Press, 2020.

McDermont, Morag, Tim Cole, Janet Newman, and Angela Piccini, eds. *Imagining Regulation Differently: Co-Creating for Engagement*. Bristol: Policy Press, 2020.

McKiernan, Erin C. "Imagining the 'Open' University: Sharing Scholarship to Improve Research and Education." *PLOS Biology* 15, no. 10 (2017): e1002614. https://doi.org/10.1371/journal.pbio.1002614.

McKiernan, Gerry. "E-Print Servers." *Science and Technology Libraries* 20, no. 2–3 (2001): 149–58. https://doi.org/10.1300/J122v20n02_13.

McLaughlin, Jeremy L. "A New Open Humanities: Introduction." *Bulletin of the Association for Information Science and Technology* 43, no. 5 (2017): 12–15. https://doi.org/10.1002/bul2.2017.1720430504.

Milojević, Staša. "Principles of Scientific Research Team Formation and Evolution." *Proceedings of the National Academy of Sciences (PNAS)* 111, no. 11 (2014): 3984–9. https://doi.org/10.1073/pnas.1309723111.

Ministry of Education, Culture and Science, Government of the Netherlands. "Amsterdam Call for Action on Open Science." 2016. https://www.government.nl/documents/reports/2016/04/04/amsterdam-call-for-action-on-open-science.

Moed, Henk F., and Gali Halevi. "Multidimensional Assessment of Scholarly Research Impact." *Journal of the Association for Information Science and Technology* 66, no. 10 (2015): 1988–2002. https://doi.org/10.1002/asi.23314.

Moore, Samuel, Cameron Neylon, Martin Paul Eve, Daniel Paul O'Donnell, and Damian Pattinson. "'Excellence R Us': University Research and the Fetishisation of Excellence." *Palgrave Communications* 1, no. 3 (2017): art. 16105. https://doi.org/10.1057/palcomms.2016.105.

Morriello, Rossana. "How Bibliometrics Is Affecting SSH." In *Proceedings of the ICTeSSH 2021 Conference*, July 20, 2021. https://doi.org/10.21428/7a45813f.16c632d9.

Mounier, Pierre. "'Publication Favela' or Bibliodiversity?: Open Access Publishing Viewed from a European Perspective." *Learned Publishing* 31, no. S1 (2018): 299–305. https://doi.org/10.1002/leap.1194.

Murphy, Mark, and Cristina Costa. "Digital Scholarship, Higher Education and the Future of the Public Intellectual." *Futures* 111 (2019): 205–12. https://doi.org/10.1016/j.futures.2018.04.011.

Murray-Rust, Peter, Cameron Neylon, Rufus Pollock, and John Wilbanks. "Panton Principles for Open Data in Science." February 19, 2010. http://pantonprinciples.okfn.org/.

Narayan, Bhuva, and Edward Luca. "Issues and Challenges in Researchers' Adoption of Open Access and Institutional Repositories: A Contextual Study of a University Repository." *Information Research* 22, no. 4 (2017). http://informationr.net/ir/22-4/rails/rails1608.html.

Narayan, Bhuva, Edward J. Luca, Belinda Tiffen, Ashley England, Mal Booth, and Henry Boateng. "Scholarly Communication Practices in Humanities and Social Sciences: A Study of Researchers' Attitudes and Awareness of Open Access." *Open Information Science* 2, no. 1 (2018): 168–80. https://doi.org/10.1515/opis-2018-0013.

Neff, Mark W. "How Academic Science Gave Its Soul to the Publishing Industry." *Issues in Science and Technology* 36, no. 2 (2020): 35–43.

Neylon, Cameron. "As a Researcher … I'm a Bit Bloody Fed Up with Data Management." *Science in the Open* (blog), June 16, 2017. https://cameronneylon.net/blog/as-a-researcher-im-a-bit-bloody-fed-up-with-data-management/.

Neylon, Cameron, Michelle Willmers, and Thomas King. "Rethinking Impact: Applying Altmetrics to Southern African Research." *Scholarly Communication in Africa: Rethinking Impact* (January 2014). https://open.uct.ac.za/bitstream/handle/11427/2285/SCAP_Neylon_RethinkingImpact_2014.pdf?sequence=1&isAllowed=y.

Neylon, Cameron, Rene Belsø, Magchiel Bijsterbosch, Bas Cordewener, Jérôme Foncel, Sascha Friesike, Aileen Fyfe, Neil Jacobs, Matthias Katerbow, Mikael Laakso, and Laurents Sesink. *Open Scholarship and the Need for Collective Action*. Edited by Cameron Neylon. Zenodo, 2019. https://doi.org/10.5281/zenodo.3454688.

Oberländer, Anja, and Torsten Reimer, eds. "Open Access and the Library." *Publications* 7, no. 1 (2019): art. 3. https://doi.org/10.3390/publications7010003.

Ochsner, Michael, Sven E. Hug, and Hans-Dieter Daniel. "Humanities Scholars' Conceptions of Research Quality." In *Research Assessment in the Humanities: Towards Criteria and Procedures*, edited by Michael Ochsner, Sven E. Hug, and Hans-Dieter Daniel, 43–69. Cham, Switzerland: Springer, 2016. https://doi.org/10.1007/978-3-319-29016-4_5.

Odell, Jere, Heather Coates, and Kristi Palmer. "Rewarding Open Access Scholarship in Promotion and Tenure: Driving Institutional Change." *College and Research Libraries News* 77, no. 7 (2016): 322–5. https://doi.org/10.5860/crln.77.7.9518.

OECD. *OECD Principles and Guidelines for Access to Research Data from Public Funding*. Paris: OECD, 2007. https://www.oecd.org/sti/inno/38500813.pdf.

Okune, Angela, Rebecca Hillyer, Leslie Chan, Denisse Albornoz, and Alejandro Posada. "Whose Infrastructure?: Towards Inclusive and Collaborative Knowledge Infrastructures in Open Science." In *Connecting the Knowledge Commons: From Projects to Sustainable Infrastructure*, edited by Leslie Chan and Pierre Mounier, https://books.openedition.org/oep/9072. Marseille: OpenEdition Books, 2019.

Oldenburg, Henry, ed. "Introduction." *Philosophical Transactions of the Royal Society* 1, no. 1 (1665): 1–2.

Open Government Partnership. "Open Government Declaration." September 2011. https://www.opengovpartnership.org/process/joining-ogp/open-government-declaration/.

Open Scholarship Initiative. "Plan A." OSI's Plan A, April 20, 2020. https://plan-a.world/.

Ortega, José Luis. "Disciplinary Differences of the Impact of Altmetric." *FEMS Microbiology Letters* 365, no. 7 (2018): fny049. https://doi.org/10.1093/femsle/fny049.

Peekhaus, Wilhelm, and Nicholas Proferes. "How Library and Information Science Faculty Perceive and Engage with Open Access." *Journal of Information Science* 41, no. 5 (2015): 640–61. https://doi.org/10.1177/0165551515587855.

Perakakis, Pandelis, and Michael Taylor. "Academic Self-Publishing: A Not-So-Distant Future." *Prometheus: Critical Studies in Innovation* 31, no. 3 (2013): 257–63. https://doi.org/10.1080/08109028.2014.891712.

Pinfield, Stephen. "Making Open Access Work: The 'State-of-the-Art' in Providing Open Access to Scholarly Literature." *Online Information Review* 39, no. 5 (2015): 604–36. https://doi.org/10.1108/OIR-05-2015-0167.

Pisa Declaration on Policy Development for Grey Literature Resources. "Pisa Declaration on Policy Development for Grey Literature Resources." May 16, 2014. http://www.greynet.org/images/Pisa_Declaration,_May_2014.pdf.

Piwowar, Heather. "Altmetrics: Value All Research Products." *Nature* 493, no. 7431 (2013): 159. https://doi.org/10.1038/493159a.

Poynder, Richard. "Preface." In *Open Divide: Critical Studies on Open Access*, edited by Joachim Schöpfel and Ulrich Herb, 1–6. Sacramento, CA: Library Juice Press, 2018.

Priem, Jason. "Altmetrics." In *Beyond Bibliometrics: Harnessing Multi-Dimensional Indicators of Performance*, edited by Blaise Cronin and Cassidy Sugimoto, 263–88. Cambridge, MA: MIT Press, 2014.

Priem, Jason, and Bradley H. Hemminger. "Scientometrics 2.0: New Metrics of Scholarly Impact on the Social Web." *First Monday* 15, no. 7 (2010). https://doi.org/10.5210/fm.v15i7.2874.

Priem, Jason, Dario Taraborelli, Paul Groth, and Cameron Neylon. "Altmetrics: A Manifesto." October 26, 2010. http://altmetrics.org/manifesto.

Prpić, John, Araz Taeihagh, and James Melton. "The Fundamentals of Policy Crowdsourcing." *P & I: Policy & Internet* 7, no. 3 (2015): 340–61. https://doi.org/10.1002/poi3.102.

Raffaghelli, Juliana Elisa. "Exploring the (Missed) Connections between Digital Scholarship and Faculty Development: A Conceptual Analysis." *International Journal of Educational Technology in Higher Education* 14 (2017): art. 20. https://doi.org/10.1186/s41239-017-0058-x.

Rees, Martin. "A Longitude Prize for the Twenty-First Century." *Nature* 509, no. 7501 (2014): 401. https://doi.org/10.1038/509401a.

Ren, Xiang. "The Quandary between Communication and Certification: Individual Academics' Views on Open Access and Open Scholarship." *Online Information Review* 39, no. 5 (2015): 682–97. https://doi.org/10.1108/OIR-04-2015-0129.

Research Data Alliance International Indigenous Data Sovereignty Interest Group. "CARE Principles for Indigenous Data Governance." The Global Indigenous Data Alliance, September 2019. https://www.gida-global.org/care.

Research Excellence Framework. *Research Excellence Framework 2014: Overview Report by Main Panel D and Sub-Panels 27 to 36*. January 2015. https://www.ref.ac.uk/2014/media/ref/content/expanel/member/Main%20Panel%20D%20overview%20report.pdf.

Ridge, Mia, ed. *Crowdsourcing Our Cultural Heritage*. Farnham: Ashgate, 2014.

Riley-Reid, Trevar D. "The Hidden Cost of Digitization—Things to Consider." *Collection Building* 34, no. 3 (2015): 89–93. https://doi.org/10.1108/CB-01-2015-0001.

Rinke, Eike Mark, and Alexander Wuttke. "Open Minds, Open Methods: Transparency and Inclusion in Pursuit of Better Scholarship." *PS: Political Science & Politics* 54, no. 2 (2021): 281–4. https://doi.org/10.1017/S1049096520001729.

Robinson-Garcia, Nicolas, Thed N. van Leeuwen, and Ismael Ràfols. "Using Altmetrics for Contextualised Mapping of Societal Impact: From Hits to Networks." *Science and Public Policy* 45, no. 6 (2018): 815–26. https://doi.org/10.1093/scipol/scy024.

Robson, Eleanor. "The Clay Tablet Book in Sumer, Assyria, and Babylonia." In *Companion to the History of the Book*, 2nd ed., edited by Jonathan Rose and Simon Eliot, 1:175–90. Newark, NJ: John Wiley & Sons, 2019.

Rockwell, Geoffrey. "Crowdsourcing the Humanities: Social Research and Collaboration." In *Collaborative Research in the Digital Humanities*, edited by Marilyn Deegan and Willard McCarty, 135–54. Farnham: Ashgate, 2012.

Rodriguez, Julia E. "Awareness and Attitudes about Open Access Publishing: A Glance at Generational Differences." *Journal of Academic Librarianship* 40, no. 6 (2014): 604–10. https://doi.org/10.1016/j.acalib.2014.07.013.

Rowlands, Ian. "What Are We Measuring?: Refocusing on Some Fundamentals in the Age of Desktop Bibliometrics." *FEMS Microbiology Letters* 365, no. 8 (2018): fny059. https://doi.org/10.1093/femsle/fny059.

Rowlands, Ian, David Nicholas, Bill Russell, Nicholas Canty, and Anthony Watkinson. "Social Media Use in the Research Workflow." *Learned Publishing* 24, no. 3 (2011): 183–95. https://doi.org/10.1087/20110306.

Rowsell, Jennifer, Ernest Morrell, and Donna E. Alvermann. "Confronting the Digital Divide: Debunking Brave New World Discourses." *Reading Teacher* 71, no. 2 (2017): 157–65. https://doi.org/10.1002/trtr.1603.

Russell, Andrew L. *Open Standards and the Digital Age: History, Ideology, and Networks*. New York: Cambridge University Press, 2014.

Salvador Declaration on Open Access: The Developing World Perspective. "Salvador Declaration on Open Access: The Developing World Perspective." September 23, 2005. http://www.icml.org/public/documents/pdf/en/Dcl-Salvador-OpenAccess-en.pdf.

Sanders, Cynthia K., and Edward Scanlon. "The Digital Divide Is a Human Rights Issue: Advancing Social Inclusion through Social Work Advocacy." *Journal of Human Rights and Social Work*, no. 6 (2021): 130–43. https://doi.org/doi.org/10.1007/s41134-020-00147-9.

San Francisco Declaration on Research Assessment. "San Francisco Declaration on Research Assessment." 2013. https://sfdora.org/read/.

"São Paulo Statement on Open Access: Joint Declaration by the African Open Science Platform, AmeliCA, COAlition S, OA2020, and SciELO." May 1, 2019. https://www.coalition-s.org/wp-content/uploads/Sao-Paulo-Statement-OA-01052019.pdf.

Sarantakos, Sotirios. *Social Research*. Melbourne: Macmillan, 1993.

Sawyer, Steve. "Data Wealth, Data Poverty, Science, and Cyberinfrastructure." *Prometheus* 26, no. 4 (2008): 355–71. https://doi.org/10.1080/08109020802459348.

Scanlon, Eileen. "Digital Scholarship: Identity, Interdisciplinarity, and Openness." *Frontiers in Digital Humanities* 5, no. 3 (2018). https://doi.org/10.3389/fdigh.2018.00003.

Scanlon, Eileen. "Scholarship in the Digital Age: Open Educational Resources, Publication and Public Engagement." *British Journal of Educational Technology* 45, no. 1 (2014): 12–23. https://doi.org/10.1111/bjet.12010.

Schmidt, Birgit, Tony Ross-Hellauer, Xenia van Edig, and Elizabeth C. Moylan. "Ten Considerations for Open Peer Review [Version 1; Peer Review: 2 Approved]." *F1000Research* 7 (2018): art. 969. https://doi.org/10.12688/f1000research.15334.1.

Schnapp, Jeffrey T., and Matthew Battles. *The Library beyond the Book*. Cambridge, MA: Harvard University Press, 2014.

Scott, Joan Wallach. *Knowledge, Power, and Academic Freedom*. New York: Columbia University Press, 2019.

Severin, Anna, Matthias Egger, Martin Paul Eve, and Daniel Hürlimann. "Discipline-Specific Open Access Publishing Practices and Barriers to Change: An Evidence-Based Review [Version 2; Peer Review: 2 Approved, 1 Approved with Reservations]." *F1000Research* 7 (2020): art. 1925. https://doi.org/10.12688/f1000research.17328.2.

Showers, Ben, ed. *Library Analytics and Metrics: Using Data to Drive Decisions and Services*. London: Facet, 2015.

Siebert, Sabina, Laura M. Machesky, and Robert H. Insall. "Point of View: Overflow in Science and Its Implications for Trust." *eLife*, no. 4 (2015): e10825. https://doi.org/10.7554/eLife.10825.

Síthigh, D. Mac, and J. Sheekey. "All That Glitters Is Not Gold, but Is It Diamond?" *SCRIPTed* 9, no. 3 (2012): 274–9. https://doi.org/10.2966/scrip.090312.274.

Sivertsen, Gunnar, and Ingeborg Meijer. "Normal versus Extraordinary Societal Impact: How to Understand, Evaluate, and Improve Research Activities in Their Relations to Society?" *Research Evaluation* 29, no. 1 (2020): 66–70. https://doi.org/10.1093/reseval/rvz032.

Smith, Matthew L., and Ruhiya Kristine Seward, eds. *Making Open Development Inclusive: Lessons from IDRC Research*. Cambridge, MA: MIT Press, 2020.

Snow, Charles Percy. *The Two Cultures and the Scientific Revolution*. London: Cambridge University Press, 1959. https://doi.org/10.2307/1578601.

Souter, David. *Towards Inclusive Knowledge Societies: A Review of UNESCO's Action in Implementing the WSIS Outcomes*. Paris: UNESCO, 2010.

Spaapen, Jack, and Gunnar Sivertsen. "Assessing Societal Impact of SSH in an Engaging World: Focus on Productive Interaction, Creative Pathways and Enhanced Visibility of SSH Research." *Research Evaluation* 29, no. 1 (2020): 1–3. https://doi.org/10.1093/reseval/rvz035.

Stallman, Richard. *Free Software, Free Society: Selected Essays of Richard M. Stallman*. Boston: GNU Press, 2002.

Stallman, Richard. "The GNU Manifesto." GNU Operating System. 1985. https://www.gnu.org/gnu/manifesto.en.html.

Suarez, Michael F., and H. R. Woudhuysen, eds. *The Oxford Companion to the Book*. Oxford: Oxford University Press, 2010. https://www.oxfordreference.com/view/10.1093/acref/9780198606536.001.0001/acref-9780198606536-e-3025?rskey=gPTCVV&result=2965.

Suber, Peter. *Open Access*. Cambridge, MA: MIT Press, 2012. https://openaccesseks.mitpress.mit.edu/.

Suber, Peter. "Preface." In *Open Access and the Humanities: Contexts, Controversies and the Future*, edited by Martin Paul Eve, ix–xi. Cambridge: Cambridge University Press, 2014.

Suber, Peter. "Why Is Open Access Moving So Slowly in the Humanities? (2004)." *American Philosophical Association (APA)* (blog), June 8, 2017. https://blog.apaonline.org/2017/06/08/open-access-in-the-humanities-part-2/.

Sugimoto, Cassidy R., Sam Work, Vincent Larivière, and Stefanie Haustein. "Scholarly Use of Social Media and Altmetrics: A Review of the Literature." *Journal of the Association for Information Science and Technology* 68, no. 9 (2017): 2037–62. https://doi.org/10.1002/asi.23833.

Svensson, Patrik. "The Humanistiscope: Exploring the Situatedness of Humanities Infrastructure." In *Between Humanities and the Digital*, edited by Patrik Svensson and David Theo Goldberg, 337–53. Cambridge, MA: MIT Press, 2015.

Swijghuisen Reigersberg, Muriel. "Problematizing Digital Research Evaluation Using DOIs in Practice-Based Arts, Humanities and Social Science Research [Version 1; Peer Review: 2 Approved]." *F1000Research* 4 (2015): art. 193. https://doi.org/10.12688/f1000research.6506.1.

Te Mana Raraunga—Māori Data Sovereignty Network. "Principles of Māori Data Sovereignty." October 2018. https://www.temanararaunga.maori.nz/s/TMR-Maori-Data-Sovereignty-Principles-Oct-2018.pdf.

Tennant, Jonathan, Ritwik Agarwal, Ksenija Baždarić, David Brassard, Tom Crick, Daniel J. Dunleavy, Thomas Rhys Evans, Nicholas Gardner, Monica Gonzalez-Marquez, and Daniel Graziotin. "A Tale of Two 'Opens': Intersections between Free and Open Source Software and Open Scholarship." *SocArXiv*, March 6, 2020. https://doi.org/10.31235/osf.io/2kxq8.

Tennant, Jonathan, Jennifer Beamer, Jeroen Bosman, Björn Brembs, Neo Christopher Chung, Gail Clement, Tom Crick, Jonathan Dugan, Alastair Dunning, and David Eccles. "Foundations for Open Scholarship Strategy Development." *MetaArXiv*, January 30, 2019. https://doi.org/10.31222/osf.io/b4v8p.

Tennant, Jonathan, Neo Christopher Chung, and Tobias Steiner. "Major Socio-Cultural Barriers to Widespread Adoption of Open Scholarship." *SocArXiv*, April 6, 2020. https://doi.org/10.31235/osf.io/bth73.

Tennant, Jonathan P., Jonathan M. Dugan, Daniel Graziotin, Damien C. Jacques, François Waldner, Daniel Mietchen, Yehia Elkhatib, Lauren B. Collister, Christina

K. Pikas, Tom Crick, Paola Masuzzo, Anthony Caravaggi, Devin R. Berg, Kyle E. Niemeyer, Tony Ross-Hellauer, Sara Mannheimer, Lillian Rigling, Daniel S. Katz, Bastian Greshake Tzovaras, Josmel Pacheko-Mendoza, Nazeefa Fatima, Marta Poblet, Marios Isaakidis, Dasapta Erwin Irawan, Sébastien Renaut, Christopher R. Madan, Lisa Matthias, Jesper Nørgaard Kjær, Daniel Paul O'Donnell, Cameron Neylon, Sarah Kearns, Manojkumar Selvaraju, and Julien Colomb. "A Multi-Disciplinary Perspective on Emergent and Future Innovations in Peer Review [Version 3; Peer Review: 2 Approved]." *F1000Research* 6 (2017): art. 1151. https://doi.org/10.12688/f1000research.12037.3.

Tennant, Jonathan P., and Tony Ross-Hellauer. "The Limitations to Our Understanding of Peer Review." *Research Integrity and Peer Review* 5, no. 6 (2020). https://doi.org/10.1186/s41073-020-00092-1.

Tennant, Jonathan P., François Waldner, Damien C. Jacques, Paola Masuzzo, Lauren B. Collister, and Chris H. J. Hartgerink. "The Academic, Economic and Societal Impacts of Open Access: An Evidence-Based Review [Version 3; Peer Review: 4 Approved, 1 Approved with Reservations]." *F1000Research* 5 (2016): art. 632. https://doi.org/10.12688/f1000research.8460.3.

Tenopir, Carol, Kenneth Levine, Suzie Allard, Lisa Christian, Rachel Volentine, Reid Boehm, Frances Nichols, David Nicholas, Hamid R. Jamali, Eti Herman, and Anthony Watkinson. "Trustworthiness and Authority of Scholarly Information in a Digital Age: Results of an International Questionnaire." *Journal of the Association for Information Science and Technology* 67, no. 10 (2016): 2344–61. https://doi.org/10.1002/asi.23598.

Terras, Melissa. "Crowdsourcing in the Digital Humanities." In *A New Companion to Digital Humanities*, edited by Susan Schreibman, Ray Siemens, and John Unsworth, 420–38. Chichester: Wiley & Sons, 2016.

Terras, Melissa. "Opening Access to Collections: The Making and Using of Open Digitised Cultural Content." *Online Information Review* [Special Issue on "Open Access: Redrawing the Landscape of Scholarly Communication." Edited by G. E. Gorman and J. Rowley] 39, no. 5 (2015): 733–52. https://doi.org/10.1108/OIR-06-2015-0193.

Thelwall, Mike, and Maria M. Delgado. "Arts and Humanities Research Evaluation: No Metrics Please, Just Data." *Journal of Documentation* 71, no. 4 (2015): 817–33. https://doi.org/10.1108/JD-02-2015-0028.

Tofield, Andros. "The COALition S and Plan S: Explained—European Legislation Requiring Scientific Publications Resulting from Research Funded by Public Grants Must Be Published in Compliant Open Access Journals or Platforms from 2020." *European Heart Journal* 40, no. 12 (2019): 952–3. https://doi.org/10.1093/eurheartj/ehz105.

Toledo, Elea Giménez. "Research Assessment in Humanities and Social Sciences in Review." *Revista Española De Documentación Científica* 41, no. 3 (2018): e208. https://doi.org/10.3989/redc.2018.3.1552.

Tóth-Czifra, Erzsébet. "The Risk of Losing the Thick Description: Data Management Challenges Faced by the Arts and Humanities in the Evolving FAIR Data Ecosystem." In *Digital Technology and the Practices of Humanities Research*, edited by Jennifer Edmond, 235–66. Cambridge: Open Book, 2019. https://doi.org/10.11647/obp.0192.10.

Tóth-Czifra, Erzsébet, and Ulrike Wuttke. "Loners, Pathfinders, or Explorers? How Are the Humanities Progressing in Open Science?" *Generation R: Exploring New Ways to Research* (blog), April 24, 2019. https://genr.eu/wp/humanities-progressing-in-open-science/.

UNESCO. *UNESCO Recommendation on Open Science*. Paris: UNESCO, November 2021. https://unesdoc.unesco.org/ark:/48223/pf0000379949.locale=en.

United Nations General Assembly. "Universal Declaration of Human Rights." 217 (III) A. Paris, 1948. Article 27. https://www.un.org/en/about-us/universal-declaration-of-human-rights.

Van de Sompel, Herbert, and Carl Lagoze. "The Santa Fe Convention of the Open Archives Initiative." *D-Lib Magazine* 6, no. 2 (February 2000). http://www.dlib.org/dlib/february00/vandesompel-oai/02vandesompel-oai.html.

Veletsianos, George. *Social Media in Academia: Networked Scholars*. New York: Routledge, 2016.

Veletsianos, George, and Royce Kimmons. "Networked Participatory Scholarship: Emergent Techno-Cultural Pressures toward Open and Digital Scholarship in Online Networks." *Computers and Education* 58, no. 2 (2012): 166–89. https://doi.org/10.1016/j.compedu.2011.10.001.

Verhulst, Stefaan G., and Andrew Young. *Open Data in Developing Economies: Toward Building an Evidence Base on What Works and How*. Cape Town: African Minds, 2017.

Vincent, James. "Getty Images Bans AI-Generated Content over Fears of Legal Challenges." *The Verge*, September 21, 2022. https://www.theverge.com/2022/9/21/23364696/getty-images-ai-ban-generated-artwork-illustration-copyright.

Walter, Maggie, Tahu Kukutai, Stephanie Russo Carroll, and Desi Rodriguez-Lonebear, eds. *Indigenous Data Sovereignty and Policy*. Abingdon, Oxon: Routledge, 2021.

Watermeyer, Richard. "Public Intellectuals vs. New Public Management: The Defeat of Public Engagement in Higher Education." *Studies in Higher Education* 41, no. 12 (2016): 2271–85. https://doi.org/10.1080/03075079.2015.1034261.

Wazny, Kerri. "'Crowdsourcing' Ten Years In: A Review." *Journal of Global Health* 7, no. 2 (2017): art. 020601. https://doi.org/10.7189/jogh.07.020601.

Wen, Shao-Fang, Mazaher Kianpour, and Basel Katt. "Security Knowledge Management in Open Source Software Communities." In *Innovative Security Solutions for*

Information Technology and Communications: SECITC 2018, edited by J. L. Lanet and C. Toma, vol. 11359. Lecture Notes in Computer Science. Cham, Switzerland: Springer, 2019. https://doi.org/10.1007/978-3-030-12942-2_6.

Wiegand, Wayne A. "Libraries and the Invention of Information." In *Companion to the History of the Book*, 2nd ed., edited by Jonathan Rose and Simon Eliot, 2: 827–40. Newark, NJ: John Wiley & Sons, 2019.

Wiley, David, and Cable Green. "Why Openness in Education?" In *Game Changers: Education and Information Technologies*, edited by Diana G. Oblinger, 81–9. Boulder, CO: Educause, 2012.

Wilkinson, Mark D., Michel Dumontier, and IJsbrand Jan Aalbersberg. "The FAIR Guiding Principles for Scientific Data Management and Stewardship." *Scientific Data* 3 (2016): art. 160018. https://doi.org/10.1038/sdata.2016.18.

Willinsky, John. *The Access Principle: The Case for Open Access Research and Scholarship*. Cambridge, MA: MIT Press, 2006.

Willinsky, John. "When the Law Advances Access to Learning: Locke and the Origins of Modern Copyright." In *Reassembling Scholarly Communications: Histories, Infrastructures, and Global Politics of Open Access*, edited by Martin Paul Eve and Jonathan Gray, 83–102. Cambridge, MA: MIT Press, 2020. https://doi.org/10.7551/mitpress/11885.003.0011.

Wilsdon, James, Liz Allen, Eleonora Belfiore, Philip Campbell, Stephen Curry, Steven Hill, Richard Jones, Roger Kain, Simon Kerridge, Mike Thelwall, Jane Tinkler, Ian Viney, Paul Wouters, Jude Hill, and Ben Johnson. *The Metric Tide: Report of the Independent Review of the Role of Metrics in Research Assessment and Management*. Higher Education Funding Council for England, 2015. https://doi.org/10.13140/RG.2.1.4929.1363.

Wilson, Christopher. "Civil Society." In *The State of Open Data: Histories and Horizons*, edited by Tim Davies, Stephen B. Walker, Mor Rubinstein, and Fernando Perini, 355–66. Cape Town: African Minds, 2019.

Wouters, Paul, Zohreh Zahedi, and Rodrigo Costas. "Social Media Metrics for New Research Evaluation." In *Springer Handbook of Science and Technology Indicators*, edited by Wolfgang Glänzel, Henk F. Moed, Ulrich Baer, and Mike Thelwall, 687–713. Cham, Switzerland: Springer, 2019. https://doi.org/10.1007/978-3-030-02511-3_26.

Zalaznik, Maja. "We Cannot Have Peace without Education and Open Science." UNESCO, October 12, 2020. https://en.unesco.org/news/we-cannot-have-peace-without-education-and-open-science.

Index

Numbers in *italics* indicate figures and tables.

Academia 67
academic boards 11
academic inquiry, societal impact of 71–2
academic performance, judgment of 39
academic publishing 2, 76 n.16
   commercialization of 7, 10–11
   commercial models for 5
   journals 5, 6, 9, 10–11, 95 n.
   proliferation of 10–11
academic research, socioeconomic divide and 3–4
Académie des Science (Paris) 9
accessibility, as FAIR principle *24*
Act for the Encouragement of Learning, An (Statute of Anne) 9–10
Advanced Research Projects Agency Network 12
AI. *See* artificial intelligence
AI-generated images 110 n.3
All European Academies (ALLEA) 55
Altmetric.com 67, 68
altmetrics (alternative metrics) 6, 22, 63, 66–9
   challenges with 68
   data available for 67–8
   emphasis in 67
   open peer review and 69
   social media platforms used for 107 n.43
   vs. bibliometrics 68
"Altmetrics: A Manifesto" (Priem et al.) 66
Amazon Mechanical Turk 59
AmeliCA (Open Knowledge Non-profit Academy-Owned Open Access) 27
Amsterdam Call for Action on Open Science 27
APCs. *See* article processing charges
ARDC. *See* Australian Research Data Commons
ARPANET. *See* Advanced Research Projects Agency Network

article processing charges 15, 27, 28, 40, 52, 53
artificial intelligence 71
arXiv 14
Ashurbanipal 8
assessment
   altmetrics for 66–9
   regimes for 66
   tensions between forms of 51
AusStage 58
Austlit 58
Australian Research Data Commons 58
authorship attribution 2
authorship rights *16*, 17

Battles, Matthew 78 n.2
BBB declarations 19, 22, 46, 71. *See also* Berlin Declaration on Access to Knowledge in the Sciences and Humanities; Bethesda Statement on Open Access Publishing; Budapest Open Access Initiative
Beijing Declaration on Research Data 27
Berlin Declaration on Access to Knowledge in the Sciences and Humanities 19, 21–2, 46
Berners-Lee, Tim 12, 59
Bethesda Statement on Open Access Publishing 19, 21, 46
bibliodiversity 15, 52
bibliographic databases 53
bibliometric counts 50
bibliometric data 68
bibliometrics 6, 61, 63–4, 66
   traditional 4
   vs. altmetrics 68
big data 54, 57
biomedical community, OA values and 21
biotechnology 71
blogging 108 n.

BOAI. *See* Budapest Open Access Initiative
book processing charges 15, 27, 28, 40, 52, 53
books
 ordering of 8
 purchase price of 13
 in the sciences and humanities 94 n.21
Boyer, Ernest L. 15, 82 n.68
BPC. *See* book processing charges
Brennan, Sheila A. 102 n.97
British Library 54
Budapest Open Access Initiative 19–20, 46, 82 n.61
Bush, Vannevar 10, 11
Butterworth-Springer 11

Canadian Humanities and Social Sciences Commons (Canadian HSS Commons) 57
Canadian Institutes of Health Research 34
Cape Town Open Education Declaration 22–3
CARE principles 55
catalogs 8
CC. *See* Creative Commons
CC BY license 14
CC BY-NC-ND license 14
CC licenses *16*
Center for Open Science 53
CERN. *See* European Organization for Nuclear Research
ChatGPT 110 n.3
Chubin, Dary E. 92 n.1
citation analysis 4, 23, 39, 63–4, 95 n.26, 103 n.6
citation data 50, 61, 63
citations, reasons for 64
citizen humanities 3, 59
citizen science 3, 29, 58–9, 100 n.84
CLARIN. *See* Common Language Resources and Technology Infrastructure
cOAlition S 27, 86 n.36
COAR. *See* Confederation of Open Access Repositories
co-creation 59
collaboration, as FAIR principle *25*
collaborative networks 57

collective benefit, authority to control, responsibility, ethics (CARE) principles 55
collective intelligence 3, 59
common good 75 n.4
Common Language Resources and Technology Infrastructure 57
communal and peer engagement 59
community-based open knowledge 58–61
computers 12–13
computing, development of 10
Confederation of Open Access Repositories 34–5, 87 n.61
contextual meaning 48
Conversation, The 53
cooperative model. *See* diamond model
copyleft 13
copyright 41, 49. *See also* Creative Commons
 laws regarding 7, 9–12, 40–1
 regulation of 5
 violation of 38, 82 n.56, 89 n.9, 109 n.3
Copyright Act (UK) 91 n.27
Costa, Cristina 80 n.39
Covid-19 29, 51, 54
Creative Commons 7, 14, 53
critical analysis 47
critical infrastructure studies 100 n.81
Crossref Event Data 67
crowdfunding 29
CrowdHeritage 60
crowdsourcing 29, 59–60, 101 n.89, 102 n.106
Crowdsourcing and Citizen Science Act of 2015 (US) 65
crowd wisdom 59
cultural data, collecting and preserving 55–6
cultural divides 58
cultural heritage, denying the value of 98 n.52
culturally sensitive information 49
cultural memory, open sharing of 57
cultural protocols 55
cuneiform texts 8

DARIAH. *See* Digital Research Infrastructure for the Arts and Humanities

DARTS (discoverable, accessible, reusable, transparent, and sustainable) 3
data
  copyright not applicable to 41
  integrity of 55
  management of 5
  mining of 54
  repositories for 3
  sharing of 54–5
  sovereignty of 55
data availability statements (DAS) 55
databases 51
datasets 54
Debates in the Digital Humanities 69
deep mapping 54
democratization 15, 17
Design and Art Australia Online 58
developing countries, improving information access in 38
diamond model (OA publication model) 15
digital age, publishing in 13–15
digital divide 5, 37–8, 88 n.2, 89 n.6
digital environment, democratization of 3
digital humanities 49, 54
digital infrastructure 56–8, 110 n.2
digital libraries 3
digital platforms, for humanities publishing 53
digital preservation 91 n.19
Digital Public Library of America 54
digital publication 2
digital reappropriation 49
Digital Research Infrastructure for the Arts and Humanities 57
digital revolution 12–13
digital scholarship 4, 75 n.1
digitization 16
digitized texts 54
Directory of Open Access Books (DOAB) 53
discoverability, as FAIR principle *24*
diversity 4, 17, 94 n.24
DORA. *See* San Francisco Declaration on Research Assessment
double-blind review 68
DSI South African Research Infrastructure Roadmap (SARIR) Programme 99 n.70

editing 8
EIFL. *See* Electronic Information for Libraries
Electronic Freedom of Information Act Amendments (US) 83 n.73
Electronic Information for Libraries 35
Elsevier 11, 38, 53
English, dominance of 38, 51–2
EOSC. *See* European Open Science Cloud
e-print repositories 34
e-print servers 20
E-RIHS. *See* European Research Infrastructure for Heritage Science
ethical governance 17
Europe, multicountry partnerships in 57
Europeana 57, 60, 99 n.60
European Commission 27, 34, 35, 60, 65
European Open Science Cloud 27, 99 n.63
European Organization for Nuclear Research 12
European Research Council 34
European Research Infrastructure for Heritage Science 57, 99 n.61
evaluation, as FAIR principle *26*
exact sciences 51
external hosting 91 n.22

Facebook 107 n.43
FAIR (findable, accessible, interoperable, and reusable) principles 3, 5, *16*, 23, 40
fair dealing 92 n.27
FAIR Guiding Principles for Data Management and Stewardship 23–7
Figshare 108 n.43
F1000Prime 108 n.43
F1000 Research 69
Former Han dynasty 8
Foucault, Michel 48, 51
Fourdrinier machine 10
Freedom of Information Act (US) 83 n.73
free software movement 12–13

galleries, libraries, archives, and museums (GLAM) 41, 57
  crowdsourcing in 60
  data held in 55
Garfield, Eugene 63
Gates (Bill and Melinda) Foundation 35

Getty Images 110 n.3
gifted amateurs 58
Github 108 n.
Global Open Access Portal (UNESCO) 28
GNU General Public License 81 n.43
GNU project 13
gold options (OA publication model) 14–15, 40, 82 n.61
Google Scholar 51
gray literature *16*, 23
Great Library of Alexandria 8
green options (OA publication model) 14
Group of Twenty (G20) Hangzhou summit 27
Gutenberg, Johannes 8

Hammarfelt, Björn 95 n.26
Hanyang Time Machine (South Korea) 99 n.68
HASS (humanities, arts, and social sciences) 58
hermeneutics 48
higher education
  expansion of 10
  globalization of 71
h-index 64
Howe, Jeff 59
humanities
  academic committees favoring books over journals 50
  citation practices in 50–1
  community-based open knowledge and 59
  critical analysis and 47–8
  crowdsourcing in 59–60
  data in 49, 54–6
  datasets in 54–5
  digital content sharing in 49
  digital infrastructure for 56–8
  distinct from sciences 48
  diversity of disciplines in 49
  epistemologies of 47
  individual culture of 49, 50
  interpretivism and 47
  journals in 52–3
  less tangible results in 51
  limited OA funding for 52–3
  long-form works published in 53

  non-English works, undiscoverable 51–2
  OA and 21, 50–4
  philosophies underlying 48
  research in 5, 51, 54–5
  role of, in encouraging open scholarship 73
  scholars in, conforming to traditional publishing channels 50, 52
  scholarship issues in 5
  source materials for 49
  Web's effect on 12
Humanities Commons 57
Humanities Networked Infrastructure (HuNI; Australia) 58, 100 n.79
hypertext 10
Hypertext Transfer Protocol 12

ICT (information and communications technology) staff, barriers facing 39–40
IFLA. *See* International Federation of Library Associations and Institutions
illegal file sharing 38
impact agenda 59
impact assessment, new mechanisms for 72
impact factors 63
impact measures 64
ImpactStory (formerly Total-Impact) 67
inclusive knowledge infrastructures 100 n.80
inclusivity 4, 17
Indigenous knowledge 49, 55, 58
Indigenous Research Data Commons (Australia) 58
industrial applicability 48
infrastructure
  localized 98 n.54
  as open scholarship element 15
innovation, as FAIR principle *26*
inquiry, freedom of 17
institutional reporting and measurement 61
institutional repositories 2, 7, 14, 20, 34, 40, 56, 65
  linkage of 34
  self-archiving in 14
insurrection of subjugated knowledges 51

intellectual property 5, 40–1, 49
International Federation of Library
 Associations and Institutions 35
internet 12–13
 as medium for distributing knowledge 21, 59
 public good and 20
Internet Archive 54
Internet of Things 71
interoperability 88 n.61
interpretivism 47

Johnson (Robert Wood) Foundation 35
Journal de sçavans 9
journal impact factors 50–1
journals 4, 6, 9–10, 11, 94 n.21

Knöchelmann, Marcel 93 n.13
knowledge
 creations of, social and community-based forms of 5
 dissemination of, technology and 4
 equity in access to 22
 societies for 28, 37
Knowledge Sharing in Publishing (India) 57–8
Knowledge Unlatched 53
KSHIP. *See* Knowledge Sharing in Publishing

Language Science Press 53
LA Referencia (the Federated Network of Institutional Repositories of Scientific Publications) 28, 53
Latin America, OA publishing models in 27–8
learned societies 4, 7–11, 13
Leiden Manifesto for Research Metrics 23, 66
LIBER. *See* Ligue des Bibliotheques Européennes de Recherche—Association of European Research Libraries
libraries 7–8, 35, 78 nn.1–3
 associations for 35
 barriers facing librarians in 39–40
 budgets for 13
 digital 13

 subscriptions for 13, 14
Library of Pergamum 8
Ligue des Bibliotheques Européennes de Recherche—Association of European Research Libraries 35
LinkedIn 67
Lorentz Workshop. 23

Macmillan 11
Malatestiana Library 8
manuscripts, ordering of 8
mass collaboration 59
Maxwell, Robert 11
measurement, as open scholarship element 15
mediated access 55
Mellon (Andrew W.) Foundation 57
Memex 10
Mendeley 107 n.43
Metallica 93 n.18
Metric Tide Report 66
microblogging 108 n.
Microworkers 59
Milojević, Staša 81 n.40
misinformation, crises of 2
modeling 54
Modern Language Association 57
monographs 96 n.37
movable type 8
multilingualism 46, 51–2
multilingual research 57
Murphy, Mark 80 n.39

nanotechnology 71
Napster 93 n.18
National eResearch Collaboration Tools and Resources initiative (Australia) 100 n.79
National Institutes of Health (US) 34
National Library of Australia 54, 60
national research councils 34
National Science Foundation 10
network analysis 54
nichesourcing 60
noncommercial model. *See* diamond model

OA. *See open access listings*
OAI. *See* Open Archives Initiative

OAPEN (Open Access Publishing in European Networks) 53
Obama administration 87 n.59
OECD. *See* Organisation for Economic Co-operation and Development
OER. *See* open educational resources
OJS. *See* Open Journal Systems
OKF. *See* Open Knowledge Foundation
Oldenburg, Henry 9
OLH. *See* Open Library of Humanities
online networking services 67
open access 17
   awareness of 72
   breaking down social and economic divides 20
   commons model for 15
   definitions of 19
   ecosystem for, BOAI recommendations for 20–1
   embargo periods for, reduced 27
   global policies for 19–35
   international call for 21
   journals 2, 15, 20
   policy statements and declarations for 5
   publishing 5, 7, 12, 14, 21, 72
   skepticism about 65
   subsidies for 52–3
   unrestricted 2
Open Access Infrastructure for Research in Europe (OpenAIRE) 35, 53, 57, 99 n.62
open access movement 13
Open Access to Scientific Research (UNESCO) 28
open archives 3
Open Archives Initiative 14, 20
Open Book Publishers 53
open collections 3
Open Content Alliance 54
open data 3
OpenEdition 53
open educational resources 17, 29. 22
open electronic archives, deposits to 20
Open Government Declaration 23
open hardware 29
open humanities 4, 5, 17, 45
   culture of 49
   definitions of 47
   distinct from open science 47
   legal and technical barriers to 49
   openness frameworks for 47
   two-way 60
Open Humanities Press 53
open initiative, silos in 5
Open Journal Systems 14
open knowledge 17. *See also* open scholarship
Open Knowledge Foundation 22
Open Knowledge for Latin America and the Global South. *See* AmeliCA
Open Library of Humanities 53
open licenses 3
Open Methods 53–4
openness 1
   different understandings of 16–17
   exposing inherent biases 73
   financial elitism and 40
   motives for 2
open peer review 3, 6, 63, 68–9, 72, 109 n.59
open practices
   disincentivized 4
   publish-or-perish culture and 65
Open Preservation Foundation 91 n.19
open publishing
   irregular uptake of 4
   platforms for 56
   services 53
open research 17. *See also* open scholarship
open research data 29
Open Research Funders Group 35
Open Scholarly Communication for the Social Sciences and the Humanities in the European Research Area for Social Sciences and Humanities 57, 99 n.63
open scholarship 12, 75 n.1
   barriers to implementing 5, 42–3
   benefits of 73
   core goal of 71–2
   defined 46
   elements of 15–17
   emergence of 3, 15–17
   fostered at whole-of-system level 73–4
   global acceptance and expansion of 72
   historical context for 4–5

implementation and governance of 72
international calls for 7
online networking services and 67
overcoming barriers to 4
policies stemming from the Global North 73
principles of 1–2
success of 4
whole-of-ecosystem approach to 46, 73
worldwide transition to 3
open scholarship movement 1–2, 5, 15–17
  challenges to 37–44
  early focus of 2, 50
  FAIR principles and 23–4
  future of 74
  humanities and 46–7
  power relations and 73
  transformation of 71
open science 17, 27, 92 n.1
  defined 45, 46
  open humanities subsumed under 5
  as umbrella term for all disciplines 46
  UNESCO Recommendation on Open Science 28–34, 46, 52
open society 1–2, 17
Open Society Foundations 35
open source code 29
open source software 13, 29
OPERAS. *See* Open Scholarly Communication for the Social Sciences and the Humanities in the European Research Area for Social Sciences and Humanities
ORCID (Open Researcher and Contributor ID) 34, 87 n.60
ORFG. *See* Open Research Funders Group
Organisation for Economic Co-operation and Development 22
orphan works 55
OS. *See* open science
OSS. *See* open source software
Oxford English Dictionary 58

Pacific and Regional Archive for Digital Sources in Endangered Cultures 58
Panton Principles for Open Data in Science 22
paper
  cost of 10
  making of 7, 10
papyrus rolls 8
PARADISEC. *See* Pacific and Regional Archive for Digital Sources in Endangered Cultures
parchment 8
participatory practice 59
participatory science 29
password protection 55
peer review 9, 11, 49
  open 3, 6, 63, 68–9, 72
  value of 69
Pergamon Press 11
permission culture 14
philanthropic organizations 35
Philosophical Transactions 9
Pisa Declaration 23
Plan S 27, 34, 71
platinum model. *See* diamond model
PLOS. *See* Public Library of Science
PLOS Article-Level Metrics 67
PLOS ONE 52
Plum Analytics 67–8
pluralistic knowledge societies 28
POSI. *See* Principles of Open Scholarly Infrastructure
positivism 47
postprints 14
pragmatism 15
predatory publishers 52
preprints 14
Principles and Guidelines for Access to Research Data from Public Funding (OECD) 22
Principles of Open Scholarly Infrastructure 56, 99 n.55
printing monopolies 10
printing technology 7, 8, 10
Project Gutenberg 13
publication. *See also* journals
  conservative cultural nature of 52
  in the digital age 13–15
  strategy for, generational approaches to 90 n.16
  traditional metrics for 4, 39
public domain 41
public engagement 102 n.97
public good 15, 17, 20, *26*, 28

Public Knowledge Project 14
Public Library of Science 20, 52
publish-or-perish culture 65
publish and read agreements 27

quality assurance 25, 49
quantum theory 71

read and publish agreements 27
Recommendation on Open Educational Resources (UNESCO) 28
Redalyc (Red de Revistas Científicas de América Latina, y El Caribe, Espana y Portugal) 27
Reddit 108 n.
REF. *See* UK Research Excellence Framework
reference management 107 n.43
Ren, Xiang 76 n.16
replicability 48
repositories 91 n.24
reproducibility, as FAIR principle 24
research
  assessment of, diversification in 6
  government funding of 10
  growth and globalization of sector 71
  impact of, new measurements for 65
  professionalization of 10
  societal benefits of 5–6
  universal access to 3
  universities' involvement in 11
ResearchBlogging 108 n.
Research Councils of the United Kingdom 34
ResearchGate 67, 107 n.43
reusability 24, 48
Rijksmuseum 99 n.66
robotics 71
Royal Society of London for Improving Natural Knowledge 9

SADiLaR (South Africa) 99 n.70
Sage 38
Salvador Declaration on Open Access 22
San Francisco Declaration on Research Assessment 23, 66
São Paulo Statement on Open Access 27
Schnapp, Jeffrey T. 78 n.2
scholarly communication 76 n.16
  changes in 7, 17, 71
  conventional model of 2
  extending audience for 2
  international principles of 17
  journals and 9
  key events in 30–3
Scholarly Publishing and Academic Resources Coalition 14
scholarly work, evaluating 64–6
scholarship, openness in 17
scholarship of engagement 82 n.68
SciELO (Scientific Electronic Library Online network) 27, 35, 53
Science 63
Science Citation Index 63
Science: The Endless Frontier (Bush) 10
sciences
  bibliometric counts in 50
  citation practices in 50
  costs in, for research and publication 53
  distinct from humanities 48, 50–2
  epistemologies, of 47
  more highly represented in open publishing 52
  team research in 80 n.40
scientific volunteering 29
Sci-Hub 89 n.9
Scopus 51, 95 n.26
scribes 8
second-language delivery 51–2
self-archiving 14, 40, 65
single-blind review 68
Sloan (Alfred P.) Foundation 35
Snow, C. P. 47, 48, 93 n.9
social bookmarking 107 n.43
social data sharing 108 n.
social media, use of, linking with societal influence 68
social networking 107 n.43
social recommending 108 n.
social scholarship 3
Social Sciences Research Network 53
social web
  scholarly communication on 66–7
  usage analysis 23
societal divides 58
societal impact 5–6
  academic inquiry and 71–2
  lacking standard for assessing 68

socioeconomic divide 3
software, free distribution of 13
source code, sharing of 12–13
source criticism 48
South African Centre for Digital Language Resources (SADiLaR) 57
SPARC. *See* Scholarly Publishing and Academic Resources Coalition
Springer 38
staff education, commitment to 72
stakeholders, role of, in promoting open practices 43–4
Stallman, Richard 12–13
Statute of Anne 9–10
STEM fields (science, technology, engineering, and mathematics) 46
Suber, Peter 94 n.21
subscription fees, OA model and 15
surveillance 71
"Sustainable and FAIR Data Sharing in the Humanities" (Maryl et al.) 55

Taylor and Francis 11, 38
team research 81 n.40
telecommunications, development of 10
text encoding 54
textual criticism 8
3D printing 71
Time-Layered Cultural Map (Australia) 58
Time Machine 57
TLCMap. *See* Time-Layered Cultural Map
Toledo, Elea Giménez 94 n.24
Total-Impact. *See* ImpactStory
Transcribe Bentham 60
transformative agreements 27
transitional agreements 27
transparency 15, 17, *25*, 48
Tri-Agency Open Access Policy on Publications (Canada) 34
Trove (National Library of Australia) 60, 96 n.39
Twitter 108 n.
two cultures divide 47–8, 56

Ubiquity Press 53
UK Research Excellence Framework 65
understandability, as FAIR principle *25*
UNESCO 28
   Recommendation on Open Science 19, 28–34, 46, 52
   Recommendation on Science and Scientific Researchers 28
United Nations Declaration of Human Rights 38
United Nations Educational, Scientific and Cultural Organization. *See* UNESCO
universities
   as early adopters of computers 12
   assessment processes at, changes in 65
   career progression at 64–5
   cultural change in 38–9
   libraries of 11
   librarians in, as advocates for open practices 39
   presses of 10–11
   promoting OA policies 72
Unix 12, 13
UN Millennium Development Goals 22, 85 n.22
user-powered systems 59
user rights 17

validated progress, as FAIR principle *26*
Vienna Principles 23
visualization 54

Web of Science 51, 95 n.
Weibo 108 n.
Wikipedia 60, 108 n.
wikis 108 n.
Wiley-Blackwell 38
Wordpress 108 n.
workflow lifecycle 48–9
World Wide Web 12, 80 n.39

Zooniverse 59
Zotero 107 n.43

www.ingramcontent.com/pod-product-compliance
Lightning Source LLC
Chambersburg PA
CBHW052129300426
44116CB00010B/1835